PUBLISHED IN 2024 BY WELBECK CHILDREN'S BOOKS
An imprint of Hachette Children's Group
Part of Hodder & Stoughton Limited
Carmelite House, 50 Victoria Embankment, London, EC4Y 0DZ
An Hachette UK Company
www.hachette.co.uk
www.hachettechildrens.co.uk

Design and layout © Welbeck Children's Books 2025
Text copyright © Welbeck Children's Books 2025

All statistical data and player heat maps provided by Opta, under license from Stats Perform.

All rights reserved. This book is sold subject to the condition that it may not be reproduced, stored in a retrieval system or transmitted in any form or by any means, electronic, mechanical, photocopying, recording or otherwise without the publisher's prior consent.

DISCLAIMER
All trademarks, brands, company names, team names, registered names, individual names, products, logos and catchphrases used or cited in this book are the property of their respective owners and used in this book for informational and identifying purposes only. This book is a publication of Welbeck Children's Books and has not been licensed, approved, sponsored or endorsed by any person or entity.

10 9 8 7 6 5 4 3 2 1
ISBN 978 1 80453 859 3

Printed and bound in Dubai
Author: David Ballheimer
Senior Commissioning Editor: Suhel Ahmed
Design Manager: Matt Drew
Picture research: Paul Langan
Production: Melanie Robertson

PICTURE CREDITS
The publishers would like to thank the following sources for their kind permission to reproduce the pictures in this book.

ALAMY STOCK PHOTO: UPI 33
GETTY IMAGES: AC Milan 52; Robin Alam/ISI Photos 47; Ion Alcoba/Quality Sport Images 56; Eric Alonso/UEFA 9; Emilio Andreoli 20; ANP 37, 55, 72; Franco Arland/UEFA 35; Matias Baglietto/NurPhoto 46; Lars Baron 57; Robbie Jay Barratt/AMA 67, 98; James Baylis/AMA 109T; Giuseppe Bellini 17; Berengui/DeFodi Images 8; John Berry 21, 88; Bagu Blanco/Pressinphoto/Icon Sport 10; Mark Blinch 60; Stefan Brauer/DeFodi Images 106T; Megan Briggs 74; Rico Brouwer/Soccrates 13; Clive Brunskill 12; David S. Bustamante/Soccrates 22, 65, 78; Pedro Castillo/Real Madrid 34; Jean Catuffe 16, 82, 100; Tim Clayton/Corbis 39; Gareth Copley 106B; Oscar Del Pozo/AFP 111T; Sebastian El-Saqqa - firo sportphoto 18; Paul Ellis/AFP 85, 109B, 110T; Gualter Fatia 62; Jacques Feeney/Offside 77; Johnny Fidelin/Icon Sport 83; Franck Fife/AFP 27; Stu Forster 105; Stuart Franklin 90, 99; Sebastian Frej/MB Media 64; Edith Geuppert/GES Sportfoto 38; James Gill/Danehouse 81; GSI/Icon Sport 50; Stefano Guidi 102; Lionel Hahn 108T; Alexander Hassenstein 95; Mike Hewitt 59; Elie Hokayem/Saudi Pro League 19; Mario Hommes/DeFodi Images 49; Image Photo Agency 42, 110B; Catherine Ivill 11; Fareed Kotb/Anadolu 48; Roland Krivec/DeFodi Images 31; Harry Langer/DeFodi Images 24; Alex Livesey 63, 89, 103; Stuart MacFarlane/Arsenal FC 54, 107T; Angel Martinez 26, 61; Stefan Matzke — sampics 43; Wagner Meier 29; Doug Murray/Icon Sportswire 28; Rene Nijhuis/MB Media 75; Mattia Ozbot/Inter 23; Alex Pantling 40; Octavio Passos 97; Ryan Pierse 101; Andrew Powell/Liverpool FC 7; Antonio Pozo/Pressinphoto/Icon Sport 68; Pressinphoto/Icon Sport 44; Joe Prior/Visionhaus 15, 51; ProShots 111B; Quality Sport Images 14, 87, 96; Michael Regan 86, 107B; Maciej Rogowski/Eurasia Sport Images 92; Fran Santiago 70; Oli Scarff/AFP 6; Silas Schueller/DeFodi Images 86; Juan Manuel Serrano Arce 1000; Justin Setterfield 93; Alexandre Simoes/Borussia Dortmund 00; Nick Tre. Smith/Icon Sportswire 25; Boris Streubel 73, 91; Justin Tallis/AFP 53; Omar Vega 94; VI Images 80; Pedro Vilela 76; Visionhaus 41, 45, 66, 71, 79; Damjan Zibert/Soccrates 30

Every effort has been made to acknowledge correctly and contact the source and/or copyright holder of each picture; any unintentional errors or omissions will be corrected in future editions of this book.

All facts and stats correct as of July 2025

STATS • PROFILES • TOP PLAYERS

WELBECK
CHILDREN'S BOOKS

CONTENTS

HOW TO USE THIS BOOK 5

DEFENDERS 6
- David Alaba 8
- Trent Alexander-Arnold 9
- César Azpilicueta 10
- Rúben Dias 11
- Virgil van Dijk 12
- Jeremie Frimpong 13
- José Giménez 14
- Joško Gvardiol 15
- Achraf Hakimi 16
- Theo Hernández 17
- Joshua Kimmich 18
- Aymeric Laporte 19
- Giovanni di Lorenzo 20
- Marquinhos 21
- Nahuel Molina 22
- Benjamin Pavard 23
- Andrew Roberston 24
- Antonee Robinson 25
- Antonio Rüdiger 26
- William Saliba 27
- Georgio Scalvini 28
- Thiago Silva 29
- Milan Škriniar 30
- Dayot Upamecano 31

MIDFIELDERS 32
- Jude Bellingham 34
- Kevin de Bruyne 35
- Emre Can 36
- Eduardo Camavinga 37
- Alphonso Davies 38
- Ousmane Dembele 39
- Bruno Fernandes 40
- Enzo Fernández 41
- Youssouf Fofana 42
- İlkay Gündoğan 43
- Frenkie de Jong 44
- Jorginho 45
- Alexis Mac Allister 46
- Weston McKennie 47
- Luka Modrić 48
- Thomas Müller 49
- Jamal Musiala 50
- Cole Palmer 51
- Christian Pulisic 52
- Declan Rice 53
- Bukayo Saka 54
- Leroy Sané 55
- Axel Witsel 56
- Granit Xhaka 57

FORWARDS 58
- Jonathan David 60
- Memphis Depay 61
- João Félix 62
- Phil Foden 63
- Olivier Giroud 64
- Antoine Griezmann 65
- Erling Haaland 66
- Alexander Isak 67
- Luka Jović 68
- Harry Kane 69
- Robert Lewandowski 70
- Ademola Lookman 71
- Romelu Lukaku 72
- Kylian Mbappé 73
- Lionel Messi 74
- Álvaro Morata 75
- Neymar 76
- Marcus Rashford 77
- Cristiano Ronaldo 78
- Mohamed Salah 79
- Son Heung-min 80
- Vinícius Júnior 81
- Nico Williams 82
- Lamine Yamal 83

GOALKEEPERS 84
- Alisson 86
- Thibaut Courtois 87
- Gianluigi Donnarumma 88
- Ederson 89
- Péter Gulácsi 90
- Lukas Hradecky 91
- Mike Maignan 92
- Emiliano Martínez 93
- Keylor Navas 94
- Manuel Neuer 95
- Jan Oblak 96
- Rui Patrício 97
- Jordan Pickford 98
- David Raya 99
- Brice Samba 100
- Robert Sanchez 101
- Yann Sommer 102
- Wojciech Szczęsny 103

MANAGERS 104
- Xabi Alonso 106
- Carlo Ancelotti
- Mikel Arteta 107
- Unai Emery
- Luis Enrique 108
- Hansi Flick
- Gian Piero Gasperini 109
- Pep Guardiola
- Eddie Howe 110
- Simone Inzaghi
- Diego Simeone 111
- Arne Slot

HOW TO USE THIS BOOK

Welcome to *Men's Football Legends 2026* — the exciting book packed with the performance stats of the biggest stars in the world of football today! We have chosen more than 100 players and managers who are (or have been) superstars in the world's top five leagues: the Bundesliga in Germany, La Liga in Spain, France's Ligue 1, the Italian Serie A and the English Premier League. The players are either playing in or have spent the majority of their careers up until the 2024/'25 season operating in these top leagues.

We feature exclusive performance data of today's finest defenders, midfielders, forwards, goalkeepers and managers — data that can be compared to assess their impact in matches.

The types of stats featured for each position vary, because each position performs a specific role on the pitch. For example, a defender's main job is to stop the opposition from scoring, so the stats focus mainly on this part of that player's game. Likewise, a striker's tackling is not as relevant as the player's goal or assists totals. What you will find for all the players is the heat map, which shows the areas of the pitch the player focuses his play in or, with goalkeepers, whether their strengths lie in the six-yard box or playing as sweeper keepers, who are comfortable all around the penalty area.

The stats span a player's career to date, playing, in particular, for teams belonging to one of the top five European leagues. The figures have been collected from domestic league and European match appearances only, and exclude data from domestic cup, super cups or international games. This narrow data pool means that the information is instantly comparable so you can decide for yourself who truly deserves to be known as a living legend of the beautiful game.

DEFENDERS

A defender's primary role is to prevent the opposing team from scoring by protecting his own goal. There are many different types of defenders (and defensive formations too) and their positions demand different skills. Full-backs play out wide and are quick and agile; they try to stop wingers and wide midfielders from delivering crosses into the penalty area. Centre-backs are in the middle; they are often strong and tall so they can win the ball from dangerous forwards. Wing-backs are like full-backs, but they play in a more forward role and also attack like wingers. Teams sometimes use a spare defender called a 'sweeper' who plays behind the centre-backs and offers extra protection.

WHAT DO THESE STATS MEAN?

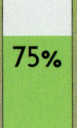
AERIAL DUELS WON
This is the percentage of headers a defender has won in his own penalty area, to interrupt an opposition attack.

INTERCEPTIONS
This is the number of times a defender has successfully stopped an attack without needing to make a tackle.

BLOCKS
A shot that is intercepted by a defender – preventing his keeper from having to make a save – counts as a block.

KEY PASSES/PASS COMPLETION
A key pass is one that results in an attacking opportunity. Pass completion indicates as a percentage the player's passing accuracy.

CLEARANCES
An attack successfully foiled, either by kicking or heading the ball away from danger, counts as a clearance.

TACKLES
This is the number of times a defender has challenged and dispossessed the opposition without committing a foul.

Did you know?

The last defender to win the Ballon d'Or, or the FIFA World's Best Player award, was Italy's Fabio Cannavaro in 2006. Only Virgil van Dijk in 2019 was voted in the top three players since 2010.

DAVID ALABA

NATIONALITY Austria
CURRENT CLUB Real Madrid

DATE OF BIRTH	24/06/1992
POSITION	LEFT-BACK
HEIGHT	1.80 M
PRO DEBUT	2007
PREFERRED FOOT	LEFT

Although his best position is left-back, David Alaba's strength is his versatility. Superb with his positioning and reading of the game, his pace and athleticism also allow him to break up attacks quickly and put his team onto the front foot.

- APPEARANCES 497
- INTERCEPTIONS 607
- GOALS 34
- TACKLES 591
- CLEARANCES 690
- PASSES 29,341
- PENALTIES SCORED 3
- BLOCKS 143
- AERIAL DUELS WON 49.4%
- PASS COMPLETION 89.2%

MAJOR CLUB HONOURS

⚽ La Liga: 2022, runner-up 2023, 2024 ⚽ Bundesliga: 2010, 2013–2021 (all B. Munich.) ⚽ UEFA Champ. League.: 2013, 2020 (all B. Munich), 2022, 2024 ⚽ FIFA Club World Cup: 2013, 2020 (all B. Munich), 2022 ⚽ Copa del Rey: 2023 ⚽ DFB-Pokal: 2013, 2014, 2016, 2019, 2020 (all B. Munich)

INTERNATIONAL HONOURS
⚽ None to date

ACTIVITY AREAS

TRENT ALEXANDER-ARNOLD

NATIONALITY England

CURRENT CLUB Real Madrid

12

Counted among the world's best overlapping defenders, Trent Alexander-Arnold plays at right-back or right wing-back. He is fast, tackles superbly and is capable of whipping in accurate crosses that strikers love to feast on! In 2025 he moved to Real Madrid, leaving Liverpool — his boyhood club — after nine years.

DATE OF BIRTH	07/10/1998
POSITION	FULL-BACK
HEIGHT	1.75 M
PRO DEBUT	2016
PREFERRED FOOT	RIGHT

- APPEARANCES 325
- BLOCKS 46
- INTERCEPTIONS 396
- PENALTIES SCORED 0
- AERIAL DUELS WON 37.8%
- PASS COMPLETION 77.9%
- GOALS 20
- PASSES 19,125
- CLEARANCES 457
- TACKLES 549

MAJOR CLUB HONOURS
⚽ Premier League: 2020, 2025 (all Liverpool) ⚽ UEFA Champions League: 2019 (Liverpool) ⚽ UEFA Champions League: runner-up 2018, runner-up 2022 (all Liverpool) ⚽ FIFA Club World Cup: 2019 (Liverpool) ⚽ FA Cup 2022 (Liverpool)

INTERNATIONAL HONOURS
⚽ UEFA Nations League: third place 2019
⚽ UEFA European Championship: runner-up 2024

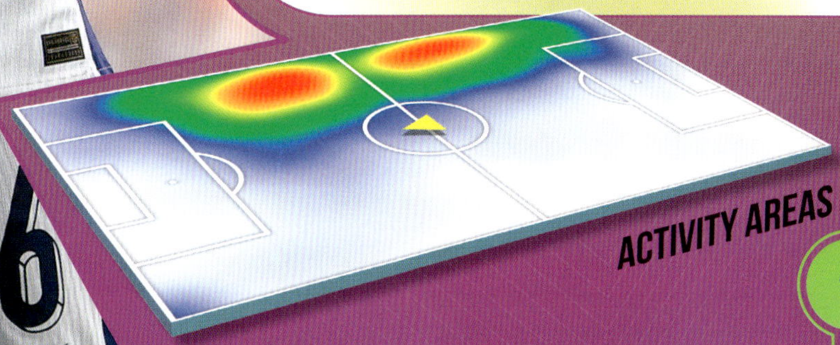

ACTIVITY AREAS

NATIONALITY
Spain

CURRENT CLUB
TBC

CÉSAR AZPILICUETA

Right-back César Azpilicueta is a natural leader, who can play anywhere on the pitch. He is excellent at using his positional sense to snuff out danger and frequently starts counter-attacks with a great right foot. At the end of the 2024/25 season, he left Atlético Madrid after two years.

DATE OF BIRTH	28/08/1989
POSITION	FULL-BACK
HEIGHT	1.78 M
PRO DEBUT	2006
PREFERRED FOOT	RIGHT

- APPEARANCES: 636
- BLOCKS: 213
- INTERCEPTIONS: 1,109
- AERIAL DUELS WON: 57.3%
- PASS COMPLETION: 82.1%
- PENALTIES SCORED: 0
- GOALS: 16
- PASSES: 31,105
- TACKLES: 1,606
- CLEARANCES: 1,911

MAJOR CLUB HONOURS
⚽ Premier League: 2015, 2017 (all Chelsea) ⚽ UEFA Champions League: 2021 (Chelsea) ⚽ UEFA Europa League: 2013, 2019 (all Chelsea) ⚽ FIFA Club World Cup: 2021, runner-up 2012 (all Chelsea) ⚽ FA Cup: 2018 (Chelsea)

INTERNATIONAL HONOURS
⚽ UEFA Nations League: runner-up 2021
⚽ FIFA Confederations Cup: runner-up 2013

ACTIVITY AREAS

RÚBEN DIAS

Although right-footed, Rúben Dias plays mainly on the left side of central defence, but is comfortable anywhere along the back line. He excels at winning challenges in the air and on the ground, making interceptions and delivering great passes over short and long distances with both feet.

NATIONALITY
Portugal

CURRENT CLUB
Manchester City

3

DATE OF BIRTH	14/05/1997
POSITION	CENTRAL
HEIGHT	1.87 M
PRO DEBUT	2015
PREFERRED FOOT	RIGHT

- APPEARANCES 212
- BLOCKS 122
- INTERCEPTIONS 191
- AERIAL DUELS WON 57.3%
- PASS COMPLETION 93%
- PENALTIES SCORED 0
- GOALS 6
- PASSES 16,737
- TACKLES 230
- CLEARANCES 539

MAJOR CLUB HONOURS
- Premier League: 2021, 2022, 2023, 2024
- UEFA Champions League: runner-up 2021, 2023
- Portuguese Premier Liga: 2019 (Benfica)
- FA Cup: 2023, runner-up 2025

INTERNATIONAL HONOURS
- UEFA Nations League: 2019

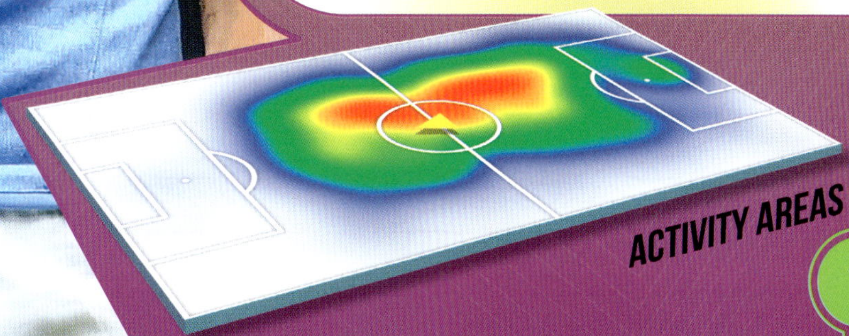

ACTIVITY AREAS

VIRGIL VAN DIJK

4

NATIONALITY Netherlands

CURRENT CLUB Liverpool

Regarded as one of the best central defenders of his generation, Virgil van Dijk's is a calm presence on the pitch which makes him a great leader. He has great positional sense and frequently breaks up attacks. He can also get on to the end of set pieces, making him dangerous in the opposition box.

DATE OF BIRTH	08/07/1991
POSITION	CENTRAL
HEIGHT	1.95 M
PRO DEBUT	2011
PREFERRED FOOT	RIGHT

- APPEARANCES 379*
- BLOCKS 201
- INTERCEPTIONS 554
- AERIAL DUELS WON 74.4%
- PASS COMPLETION 89.1%
- PENALTIES SCORED 0
- GOALS 30
- PASSES 26,695
- TACKLES 368
- CLEARANCES 1,853

*Excludes data from Scottish Premiership

MAJOR CLUB HONOURS
⚽ Premier League: 2020, 2025 ⚽ Scottish Premiership: 2014, 2015 (Celtic) ⚽ UEFA Champions League: 2019, runner-up 2018, runner-up 2022 ⚽ FIFA Club World Cup: 2019 ⚽ FA Cup: 2022

INTERNATIONAL HONOURS
⚽ UEFA Nations League: runner-up 2019

ACTIVITY AREAS

JEREMIE FRIMPONG

Jeremie Frimpong is as comfortable in midfield as he is playing as a wing-back and fits perfectly in both roles. He uses his great pace and passing ability in attacking situations, but has the technical skills to perform defensive duties. In May 2025, Frimpong joined Liverpool.

NATIONALITY
Netherlands

CURRENT CLUB
Liverpool

30

DATE OF BIRTH	10/12/2000
POSITION	RIGHT WING-BACK
HEIGHT	1.72 M
PRO DEBUT	2019
PREFERRED FOOT	RIGHT

- APPEARANCES 181*
- INTERCEPTIONS 74
- GOALS 27
- TACKLES 198
- CLEARANCES 146
- PASSES 4,993
- PENALTIES SCORED 0
- BLOCKS 15

AERIAL DUELS WON 37.8%
PASS COMPLETION 82.1%

*Excludes data from Scottish Premiership

MAJOR CLUB HONOURS
⚽ Bundesliga: 2024 (Bayer Leverkusen) ⚽ UEFA Europa League: runner-up 2024 (Bayer Leverkusen) ⚽ DFB-Pokal 2024 (Bayer Leverkusen) ⚽ Scottish Premiership: 2020 (Celtic) ⚽ Scottish Cup: 2020 (Celtic)

INTERNATIONAL HONOURS
⚽ UEFA Nations League: runner-up 2019

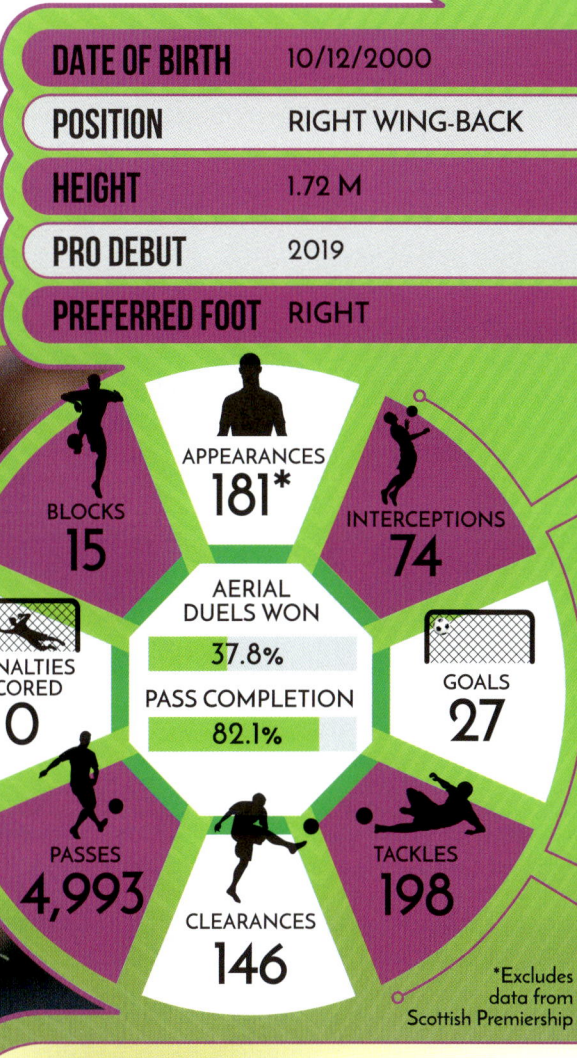

ACTIVITY AREAS

NATIONALITY
Uruguay

CURRENT CLUB
Atlético Madrid

JOSÉ GIMÉNEZ

The Uruguayan is a tough-tackling centre-back who is quick off the mark and difficult to knock off the ball. He made his international debut when he was just 19 and has also thrived at club level since joining Atlético Madrid in 2013.

DATE OF BIRTH	20/01/1995
POSITION	CENTRAL
HEIGHT	1.85 M
PRO DEBUT	2012
PREFERRED FOOT	RIGHT

- APPEARANCES: 323
- BLOCKS: 196
- INTERCEPTIONS: 471
- PENALTIES SCORED: 0
- AERIAL DUELS WON: 63.6%
- PASS COMPLETION: 84.7%
- GOALS: 10
- PASSES: 12,521
- TACKLES: 450
- CLEARANCES: 1,447

MAJOR CLUB HONOURS
⚽ La Liga: 2014, 2021 ⚽ UEFA Europa League: 2018
⚽ UEFA Super Cup: 2018 ⚽ UEFA Champions League: runner-up 2014, 2016

INTERNATIONAL HONOURS
⚽ FIFA U-20 World Cup: runner-up 2013
⚽ Copa América: third place 2024

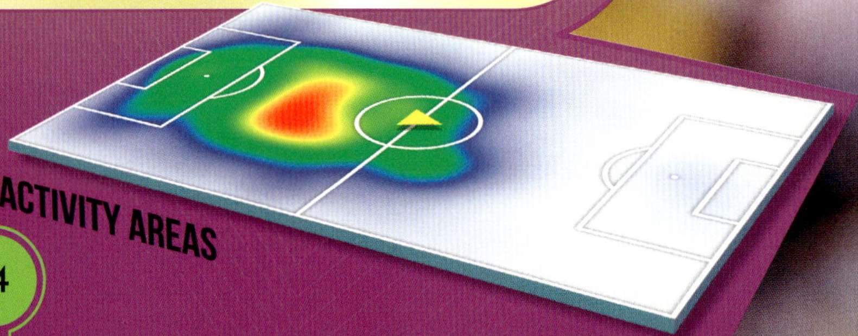

ACTIVITY AREAS

JOŠKO GVARDIOL

Joško Gvardiol is a master in one-on-one situations, knowing exactly when to block or make a tackle. He reads the game well and is clever at making interceptions. His sound technique at the back is matched by his ability to turn defence into attack.

NATIONALITY
Croatia

CURRENT CLUB
Manchester City

DATE OF BIRTH	23/01/2002
POSITION	CENTRAL
HEIGHT	1.85 M
PRO DEBUT	2019
PREFERRED FOOT	LEFT

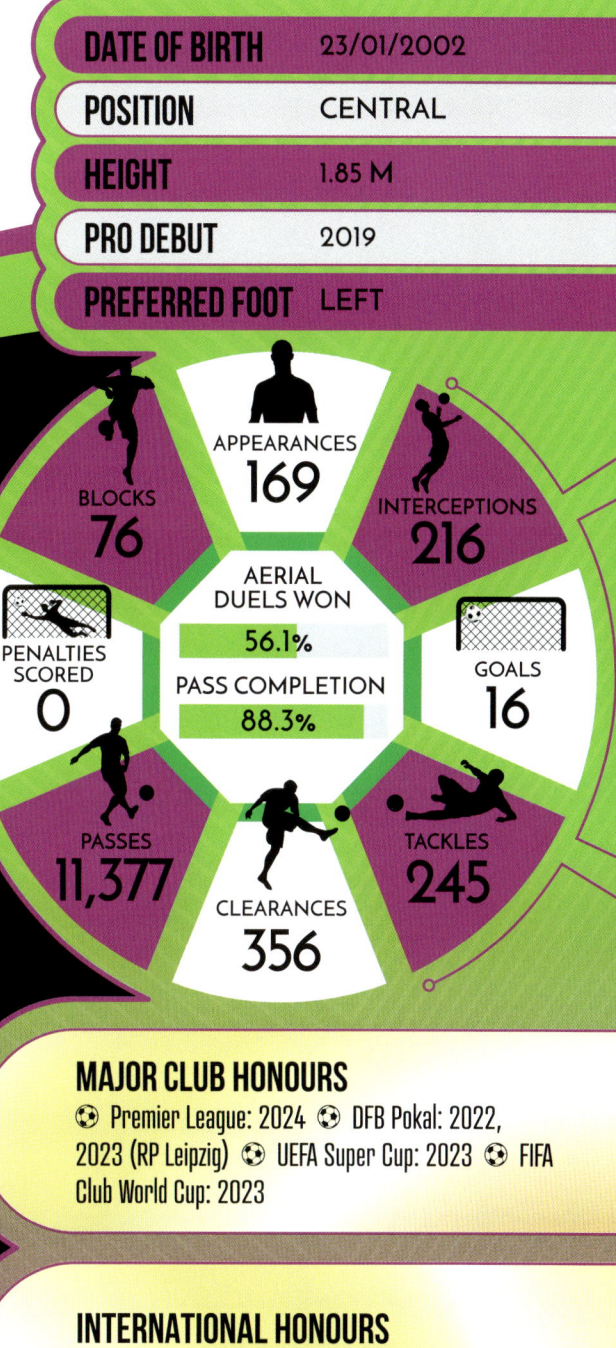

- APPEARANCES 169
- INTERCEPTIONS 216
- GOALS 16
- TACKLES 245
- CLEARANCES 356
- PASSES 11,377
- PENALTIES SCORED 0
- BLOCKS 76
- AERIAL DUELS WON 56.1%
- PASS COMPLETION 88.3%

MAJOR CLUB HONOURS

⚽ Premier League: 2024 ⚽ DFB Pokal: 2022, 2023 (RP Leipzig) ⚽ UEFA Super Cup: 2023 ⚽ FIFA Club World Cup: 2023

INTERNATIONAL HONOURS

⚽ FIFA World Cup: third place 2022
⚽ Copa América third place 2024

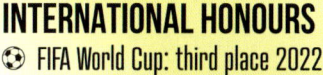

ACTIVITY AREAS

NATIONALITY
Morocco

CURRENT CLUB
Paris Saint-Germain

ACHRAF HAKIMI

Known for his versatility, Ashraf Hakimi is equally good as a right-sided wing-back as he is in midfield. His exceptional pace allows him to stop opposition attackers with clean tackles or interceptions and he can than leave opponents behind when he joins the attack.

DATE OF BIRTH	04/11/1998
POSITION	RIGHT-BACK
HEIGHT	1.81 M
PRO DEBUT	2016
PREFERRED FOOT	RIGHT

- APPEARANCES 274
- INTERCEPTIONS 238
- GOALS 42
- TACKLES 495
- CLEARANCES 232
- PASSES 15,499
- PENALTIES SCORED 0
- BLOCKS 26
- AERIAL DUELS WON 41.9%
- PASS COMPLETION 87.8%

MAJOR CLUB HONOURS
⚽ Ligue 1: 2022, 2023, 2024, 2025 ⚽ Serie A: 2021 (Inter Milan) ⚽ UEFA Champions League: 2018 (R. Madrid), 2025 ⚽ FIFA World Club Cup: 2017, runner-up 2025, (R. Madrid) ⚽ Coupe de France: 2024, 2025

INTERNATIONAL HONOURS
⚽ None to date

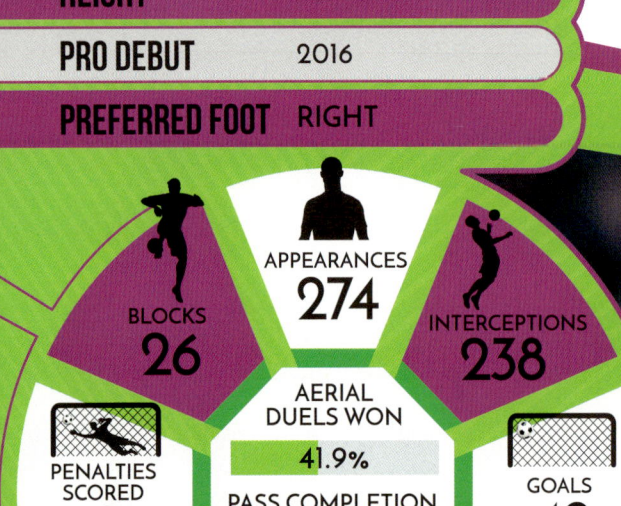

ACTIVITY AREAS

THEO HERNÁNDEZ

Known more for his attacking qualities than his defensive work, Theo Hernández (younger brother of Lucas) is a footballer who is blessed with great pace; he can dribble rapidly with the ball at his feet and get into goalscoring positions. A fan favourite at AC Milan, Hernández left the club in 2025 after five seasons.

NATIONALITY
France

CURRENT CLUB
Al Hilal (S. Arabia)

19

DATE OF BIRTH	06/10/1997
POSITION	LEFT-BACK
HEIGHT	1.84 M
PRO DEBUT	2015
PREFERRED FOOT	LEFT

APPEARANCES 312
INTERCEPTIONS 288
GOALS 34
TACKLES 476
CLEARANCES 433
PASSES 13,597
PENALTIES SCORED 4
BLOCKS 71
AERIAL DUELS WON 65%
PASS COMPLETION 84.4%

MAJOR CLUB HONOURS
⚽ Serie A: 2022 (AC Milan) ⚽ UEFA Champions League: 2018 (Real Madrid) ⚽ FIFA World Club Cup: 2017 (Real Madrid)

INTERNATIONAL HONOURS
⚽ FIFA World Cup: runner-up 2022
⚽ UEFA Nations League: 2021, third place 2025

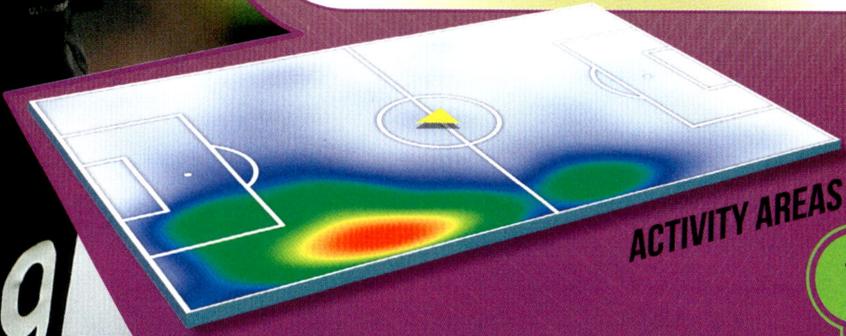

ACTIVITY AREAS

NATIONALITY
Germany

CURRENT CLUB
Bayern Munich

DATE OF BIRTH	08/02/1995
POSITION	RIGHT-BACK
HEIGHT	1.77 M
PRO DEBUT	2013
PREFERRED FOOT	RIGHT

JOSHUA KIMMICH

A top-class footballer who excels at right-back, Joshua Kimmich is also adaptable and can play in most defensive and midfield positions. He is a natural leader and communicator on the pitch with an array of skills, including positional sense, timing, anticipation, tackling, passing, heading and stamina.

- APPEARANCES: 392
- BLOCKS: 76
- INTERCEPTIONS: 424
- AERIAL DUELS WON: 44.7%
- PASS COMPLETION: 90.4%
- PENALTIES SCORED: 2
- GOALS: 41
- PASSES: 28,698
- TACKLES: 588
- CLEARANCES: 339

MAJOR CLUB HONOURS
⚽ Bundesliga: 2016, 2017, 2018, 2019, 2020, 2021, 2022, 2023, 2025 ⚽ UEFA Champions League: 2020 ⚽ DFB-Pokal: 2016, 2019, 2020 ⚽ FIFA Club World Cup: 2020

INTERNATIONAL HONOURS
⚽ FIFA Confederations Cup: 2017

ACTIVITY AREAS

AYMERIC LAPORTE

Aymeric Laporte was among Europe's best defenders before moving to the Saudi Pro League in 2023. He is a powerful tackler, excellent in the air and a good organiser at the back. Laporte can also start attacks with his precise passing out of defence.

NATIONALITY
Spain

CURRENT CLUB
Al Nassr (S. Arabia)

27

DATE OF BIRTH	27/05/1994
POSITION	CENTRAL
HEIGHT	1.89 M
PRO DEBUT	2011
PREFERRED FOOT	LEFT

- APPEARANCES 392
- INTERCEPTIONS 669
- GOALS 25
- TACKLES 599
- CLEARANCES 1,334
- PASSES 25,327
- PENALTIES SCORED 0
- BLOCKS 154
- AERIAL DUELS WON 64.9%
- PASS COMPLETION 88.7%

MAJOR CLUB HONOURS
⚽ Premier League: 2018, 2019, 2021, 2022, 2023 (all Man. City) ⚽ UEFA Champions League: runner-up 2021, 2023 (all Man. City) ⚽ FA Cup: 2019, 2023 (all Man. City)

INTERNATIONAL HONOURS
⚽ UEFA Nations League: runner-up 2021, 2023
⚽ UEFA European Championship: 2024

ACTIVITY AREAS

22

NATIONALITY
Italy

CURRENT CLUB
Napoli

GIOVANNI DI LORENZO

Although he began his professional career as an attacking player, Giovanni di Lorenzo is now an excellent defender, normally positioned at right-back, but he can play in the middle too. He has a solid tackling technique, is physically strong and possesses good aerial ability.

DATE OF BIRTH	04/08/1993
POSITION	RIGHT-BACK
HEIGHT	1.83 M
PRO DEBUT	2010
PREFERRED FOOT	BOTH

- BLOCKS: 85
- APPEARANCES: 291
- INTERCEPTIONS: 253
- AERIAL DUELS WON: 52.5%
- PASS COMPLETION: 85.9%
- PENALTIES SCORED: 0
- GOALS: 22
- PASSES: 16,478
- TACKLES: 527
- CLEARANCES: 433

MAJOR CLUB HONOURS
- Serie A: 2023, 2025
- Coppa Italia: 2020

INTERNATIONAL HONOURS
- UEFA European Championship: 2020 (2021)
- UEFA Nations League: third place 2021, 2023

ACTIVITY AREAS

20

MARQUINHOS

Marquinhos is a clever defender. He may not be a powerhouse like many of today's top-class centre-backs but has the speed, agility and intelligence to mark the quickest forwards, plus he can be very effective going forward.

NATIONALITY
Brazil

CURRENT CLUB
Paris Saint-Germain

DATE OF BIRTH	14/05/1994
POSITION	CENTRAL
HEIGHT	1.83 M
PRO DEBUT	2012
PREFERRED FOOT	RIGHT

- APPEARANCES 451
- BLOCKS 290
- INTERCEPTIONS 568
- PENALTIES SCORED 0
- AERIAL DUELS WON 57.8%
- PASS COMPLETION 92.8%
- GOALS 35
- PASSES 29,098
- CLEARANCES 1,554
- TACKLES 681

MAJOR CLUB HONOURS

⚽ Ligue 1: 2014, 2015, 2016, 2018, 2019, 2020, 2022, 2023, 2024, 2025 ⚽ UEFA Champions League: runner-up 2020, 2025 ⚽ FIFA World Club Cup: runner-up 2025 ⚽ Coupe de France: 2015, 2016, 2017, 2018, runner-up 2019, 2020, 2021, 2024, 2025

INTERNATIONAL HONOURS

⚽ Copa América: 2019, runner-up 2021
⚽ Olympic Games: 2016

ACTIVITY AREAS

NAHUEL MOLINA

16

NATIONALITY Argentina
CURRENT CLUB Atlético Madrid

Nahuel Molina has worked hard to become a dominant force on the right flank. Very quick, with fine positional sense and good tackling technique, he is also comfortable with the ball at his feet and a tremendous passer in attacking situations.

DATE OF BIRTH	06/04/1998
POSITION	RIGHT-BACK
HEIGHT	1.75 M
PRO DEBUT	2016
PREFERRED FOOT	RIGHT

- APPEARANCES 181
- INTERCEPTIONS 97
- GOALS 16
- TACKLES 258
- CLEARANCES 218
- PASSES 6,249
- PENALTIES SCORED 0
- BLOCKS 24
- AERIAL DUELS WON 39.4%
- PASS COMPLETION 78.3%

MAJOR CLUB HONOURS
- None to date

INTERNATIONAL HONOURS
- FIFA World Cup: 2022
- Copa América: 2021, 2024
- CONMEBOL–UEFA Cup of Champions: 2022

ACTIVITY AREAS

BENJAMIN PAVARD

One of the most accomplished defenders in world football, Benjamin Pavard has the ability to time his tackle perfectly and shut down opposing players in possession of the ball. He has genuine pace and can also move the ball down one or two lines of defence with an incisive pass.

NATIONALITY
France

CURRENT CLUB
Inter Milan

28

DATE OF BIRTH	28/03/1996
POSITION	CENTRAL
HEIGHT	1.86 M
PRO DEBUT	2014
PREFERRED FOOT	RIGHT

- APPEARANCES: 293
- BLOCKS: 149
- INTERCEPTIONS: 468
- PENALTIES SCORED: 0
- AERIAL DUELS WON: 60.2%
- PASS COMPLETION: 88%
- GOALS: 12
- PASSES: 17,126
- CLEARANCES: 860
- TACKLES: 414

MAJOR CLUB HONOURS
⚽ Serie A: 2024 ⚽ Bundesliga: 2020, 2021, 2022, 2023 (all B. Munich) ⚽ UEFA Champions League: 2020 (B. Munich), runner-up 2025 ⚽ FIFA Club World Cup: 2020 (B. Munich) ⚽ DFB-Pokal: 2020 (B. Munich)

INTERNATIONAL HONOURS
⚽ FIFA World Cup: 2018, runner-up 2022
⚽ UEFA Nations League: 2021, third place 2025

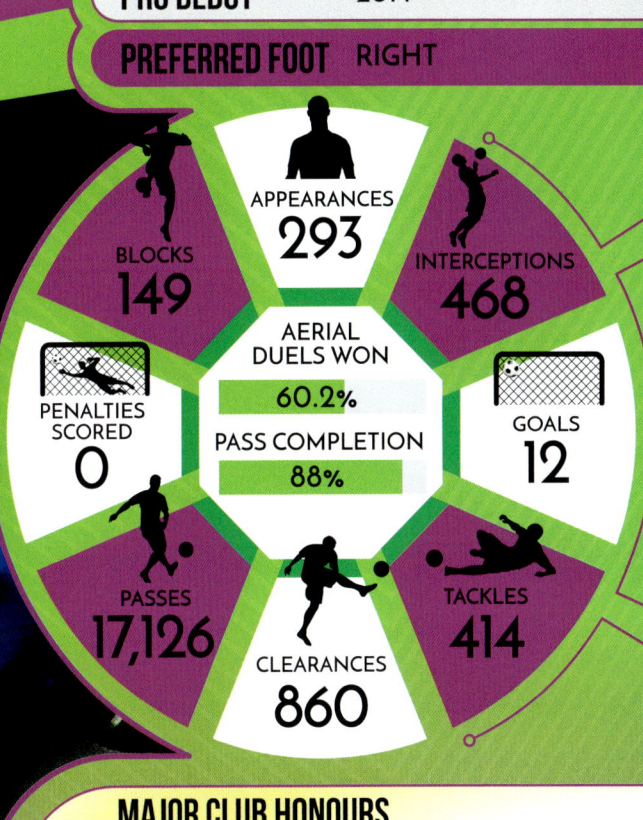

ACTIVITY AREAS

 NATIONALITY
Scotland

CURRENT CLUB
Liverpool

ANDREW ROBERTSON

Andrew Robertson has become one of the world's most reliable defenders, carrying out his duties without fuss or flashiness. Aside from his defensive skillset, he has the ability to hare down the flank, complete neat one-twos and whip over dangerous crosses, which make him an asset in attack.

DATE OF BIRTH	11/03/1994
POSITION	LEFT-BACK
HEIGHT	1.78 M
PRO DEBUT	2012
PREFERRED FOOT	LEFT

- BLOCKS: 69
- APPEARANCES: 372
- INTERCEPTIONS: 329
- AERIAL DUELS WON: 50.4%
- PASS COMPLETION: 84.1%
- PENALTIES SCORED: 0
- GOALS: 12
- PASSES: 21,032
- CLEARANCES: 627
- TACKLES: 550

MAJOR CLUB HONOURS
⚽ Premier League: 2020, 2025 ⚽ UEFA Champions League: 2019 ⚽ FIFA World Club Cup: 2019 ⚽ UEFA Super Cup: 2019 ⚽ FA Cup: 2022

INTERNATIONAL HONOURS
⚽ None to date

ACTIVITY AREAS

ANTONEE ROBINSON

An energetic and dynamic presence on the pitch, Antonee Robinson is a solid tackler and he reads the game well, consistently making timely interceptions. He has natural pace, too, and is a willing attacker, making overlapping runs and joining in attacks in the final third.

NATIONALITY	USA
CURRENT CLUB	Fulham
DATE OF BIRTH	08/08/1997
POSITION	LEFT-BACK
HEIGHT	1.83 M
PRO DEBUT	2015
PREFERRED FOOT	LEFT

- APPEARANCES: 136
- INTERCEPTIONS: 232
- AERIAL DUELS WON: 62.7%
- PASS COMPLETION: 77.4%
- GOALS: 0
- TACKLES: 295
- CLEARANCES: 362
- PASSES: 5,770
- PENALTIES SCORED: 0
- BLOCKS: 31

MAJOR CLUB HONOURS
- EFL Championship: 2022

INTERNATIONAL HONOURS
- CONCACAF Nations League: 2020, 2023, 2024

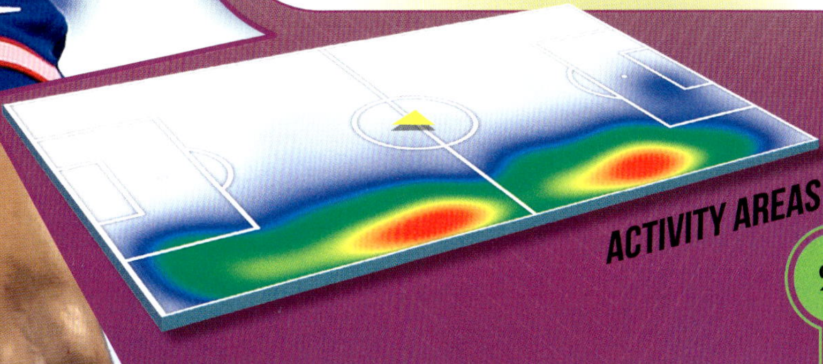

ACTIVITY AREAS

NATIONALITY
Germany

CURRENT CLUB
Real Madrid

ANTONIO RÜDIGER

Antonio Rüdiger is a dominant defender all along the back line, winning tackles with his strength and taking charge of the penalty area with his heading ability. He is also an excellent passer, reads the game well and leads by example.

DATE OF BIRTH	03/03/1993
POSITION	CENTRAL
HEIGHT	1.90 M
PRO DEBUT	2011
PREFERRED FOOT	RIGHT

- BLOCKS: 182
- APPEARANCES: 435
- INTERCEPTIONS: 394
- AERIAL DUELS WON: 59.3%
- PASS COMPLETION: 88.1%
- PENALTIES SCORED: 0
- GOALS: 19
- PASSES: 25,407
- CLEARANCES: 1,436
- TACKLES: 543

MAJOR CLUB HONOURS
⚽ La Liga: 2024 ⚽ UEFA Champions League: 2021 (Chelsea), 2024 ⚽ FIFA World Club Cup: 2021 (Chelsea), 2022 ⚽ UEFA Europa League 2019 (Chelsea) ⚽ UEFA Super Cup: 2021 (Chelsea), 2022, 2024 ⚽ FA Cup: 2018 (Chelsea) ⚽ Copa del Rey: 2023

INTERNATIONAL HONOURS
⚽ FIFA Confederations Cup: 2017

ACTIVITY AREAS

WILLIAM SALIBA

When William Saliba was just six years old he was coached by Kylian Mbappe's father, and the central defender has followed the legendary Frenchman into the national team. A solid tackler, he is a calm, solid presence in defence, with excellent timing, plus immense positional awareness.

NATIONALITY
France

CURRENT CLUB
Arsenal

DATE OF BIRTH	24/03/2001
POSITION	CENTRE-BACK
HEIGHT	1.92 M
PRO DEBUT	2018
PREFERRED FOOT	RIGHT

- APPEARANCES: 224
- INTERCEPTIONS: 229
- GOALS: 8
- TACKLES: 303
- CLEARANCES: 620
- PASSES: 15,860
- PENALTIES SCORED: 0
- BLOCKS: 100
- AERIAL DUELS WON: 60.3%
- PASS COMPLETION: 92%

MAJOR CLUB HONOURS
- Coupe de France: runner-up 2020 (PSG)

INTERNATIONAL HONOURS
- FIFA World Cup: runners-up 2022

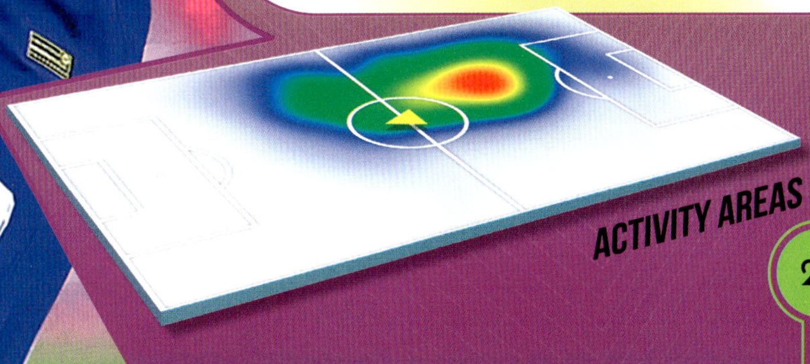

ACTIVITY AREAS

42

NATIONALITY
Italy

CURRENT CLUB
Atalanta

GEORGIO SCALVINI

A tall centre-back who is both excellent in the air and a technically sound tackler, Georgio Scalvani came to prominence in 2024, though a bad knee injury just before the EURO championship halted his rise. He is back now and many experts believe he will grow into a world-class defender.

DATE OF BIRTH	11/12/2003
POSITION	CENTRE-BACK
HEIGHT	1.94 M
PRO DEBUT	2021
PREFERRED FOOT	RIGHT

- BLOCKS: 32
- APPEARANCES: 100
- INTERCEPTIONS: 153
- AERIAL DUELS WON: 60.1%
- PASS COMPLETION: 81.7%
- PENALTIES SCORED: 0
- GOALS: 5
- PASSES: 3,996
- TACKLES: 160
- CLEARANCES: 160

MAJOR CLUB HONOURS
⚽ UEFA Europa League: 2024

INTERNATIONAL HONOURS
⚽ None to date

ACTIVITY AREAS

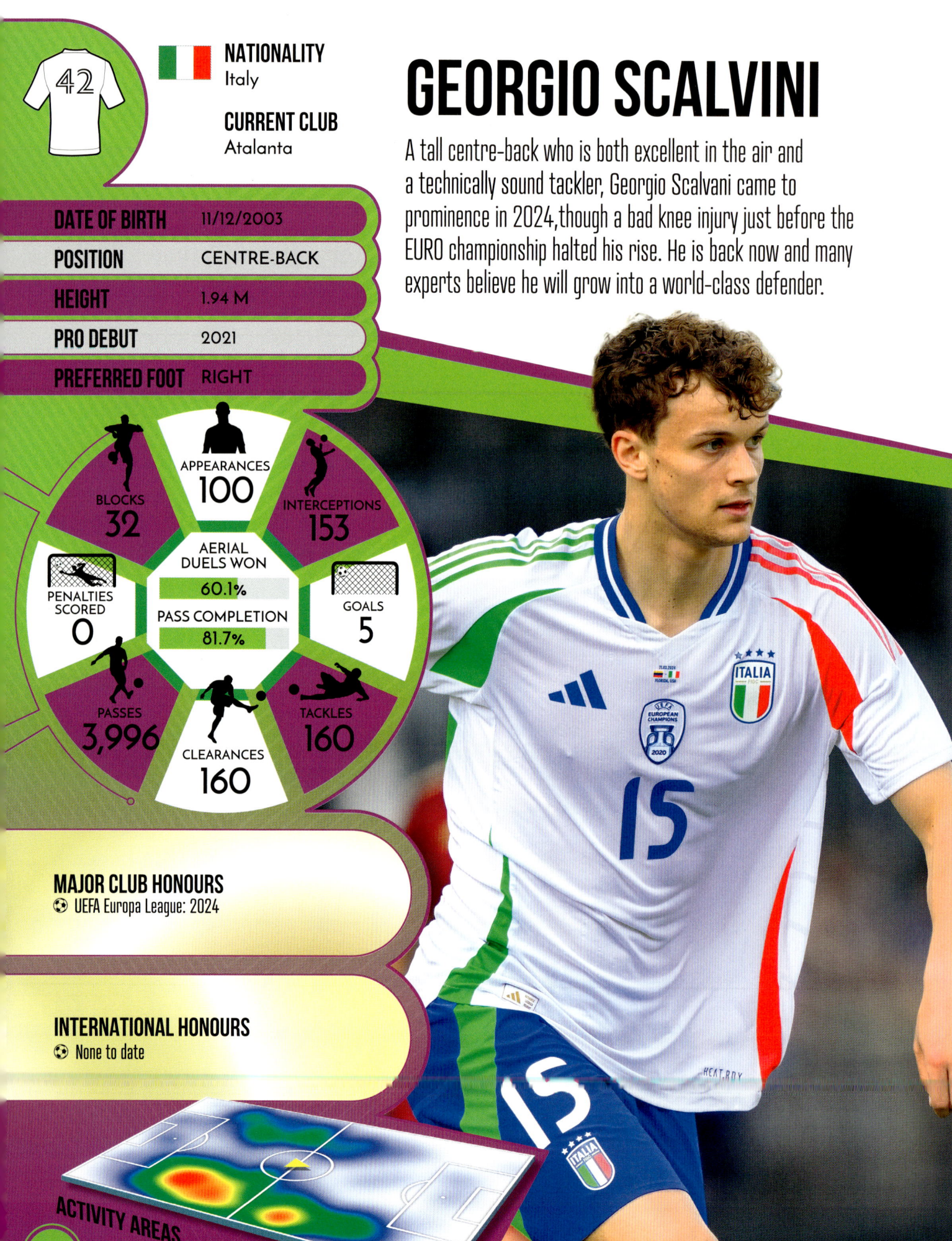

THIAGO SILVA

Thiago Silva has long been recognised as one of the world's best central defenders — some experts considering him an all-time great. A leader on the pitch, his all-around awareness ensures he is always perfectly placed to make important interventions.

NATIONALITY
Brazil

CURRENT CLUB
Fluminense (Brazil)

DATE OF BIRTH	22/09/1984
POSITION	CENTRE-BACK
HEIGHT	1.83 M
PRO DEBUT	2002
PREFERRED FOOT	RIGHT

- APPEARANCES: 556
- BLOCKS: 370
- INTERCEPTIONS: 1,064
- PENALTIES SCORED: 0
- AERIAL DUELS WON: 71.3%
- PASS COMPLETION: 92.7%
- GOALS: 27
- PASSES: 35,769
- CLEARANCES: 2,710
- TACKLES: 760

MAJOR CLUB HONOURS

⚽ UEFA Champions League: 2021 (Chelsea), runner-up 2020 (PSG) ⚽ UEFA Super Cup: 2021 (Chelsea) ⚽ FIFA Club World Cup: 2021 (Chelsea) ⚽ Serie A: 2011 (AC Milan) ⚽ Ligue 1: 2013-2020 (PSG) ⚽ Coupe de France: 2015-18, 2020 (all PSG) ⚽ FA Cup: 2022 (Chelsea)

INTERNATIONAL HONOURS

⚽ FIFA Confederations Cup: 2013
⚽ Copa América: 2019, runner-up 2021
⚽ Olympic Games: silver medal 2012, bronze medal 2008

ACTIVITY AREAS

MILAN ŠKRINIAR

37

NATIONALITY Slovakia
CURRENT CLUB Fenerbahce (Turkey)

Centre-back Milan Škriniar is a forceful tackler, strong in the air and combative on the ground. But what sets Škriniar apart are his ball-playing skills, as well as his ability to stay calm under pressure and pick out intelligent passes.

DATE OF BIRTH	11/02/1995
POSITION	CENTRE-BACK
HEIGHT	1.87 M
PRO DEBUT	2012
PREFERRED FOOT	RIGHT

- APPEARANCES: 321
- INTERCEPTIONS: 283
- GOALS: 15
- TACKLES: 500
- CLEARANCES: 1,048
- PASSES: 20,101
- PENALTIES SCORED: 0
- BLOCKS: 212
- AERIAL DUELS WON: 51.8%
- PASS COMPLETION: 92.3%

MAJOR CLUB HONOURS

⚽ Ligue 1: 2024, 2025 (PSG) ⚽ Serie A: 2021 (Inter Milan) ⚽ UEFA Champions League: runner-up 2023 (Inter Milan), 2025 ⚽ UEFA Europa League: runner-up 2020 (Inter Milan) ⚽ Coupe de France: 2024, 2025 (all PSG) ⚽ Coppa Italia: 2022, 2023 (Inter Milan)

INTERNATIONAL HONOURS

⚽ King's Cup: 2018

ACTIVITY AREAS

DAYOT UPAMECANO

Dayot Upamecano has developed into an exceptional centre-half with all the talents needed for the position. His standout talent is his ability with the ball at his feet — a quality that complements his passing accuracy.

NATIONALITY France

CURRENT CLUB Bayern Munich

DATE OF BIRTH	27/10/1998
POSITION	CENTRE-BACK
HEIGHT	1.86 M
PRO DEBUT	2015
PREFERRED FOOT	RIGHT

- APPEARANCES 284
- BLOCKS 102
- INTERCEPTIONS 412
- PENALTIES SCORED 0
- AERIAL DUELS WON 60.6%
- PASS COMPLETION 89.2%
- GOALS 8
- PASSES 19,724
- CLEARANCES 817
- TACKLES 556

MAJOR CLUB HONOURS
- Bundesliga: 2022, 2023, 2025
- DFL Supercup: 2021

INTERNATIONAL HONOURS
- UEFA Nations League: 2021
- FIFA World Cup: runner-up 2022

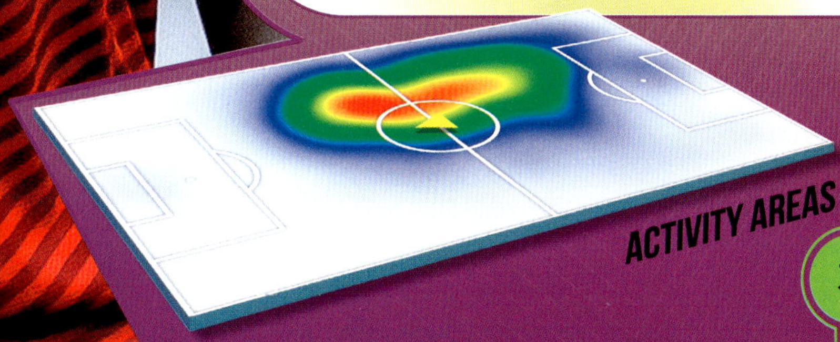

ACTIVITY AREAS

MIDFIELDERS

Midfielders are the heartbeat of a team. Not only do they play between the forwards and the defenders, but they also help out their team-mates at both ends. Midfielders fall into one of four main categories: 1) defensive midfielders, who sit in front of the back four and are great tacklers; 2) the attacking full-backs operating on the wings, who whip crosses into the box; 3) the central midfielders, who are brilliant at setting up and then joining attacks, as well as helping out in defence whenever needed; 4) the playmakers — these are the stars who build the attack with their creative play.

WHAT DO THE STATS MEAN?

ASSISTS
A pass, cross or header to a team-mate who then scores counts as an assist. This stat also includes a deflected shot that is converted by a team-mate.

SHOTS
Any deliberate strike on goal counts as a shot. The strike does not have to be on target or force a save from the keeper.

CHANCES CREATED
Any pass that results in a shot at goal (whether or not the goal is scored) is regarded as a chance created.

TACKLES
This is the number of times the player has challenged and dispossessed the opposition without committing a foul.

DRIBBLES
This is the number of times the player has gone past an opponent while running with the ball.

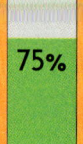
SUCCESSFUL PASSES
75%
This shows as a percentage how successful the midfielder is at finding team-mates with passes, whether over 5 or 60 metres.

Did you know?

Midfielders tend to do the most running in a game. "Box to box" central midfielders will cover between 9.5 and 12 km (more than a quarter of a marathon) over 90 minutes.

 5

 **NATIONALITY**
England

CURRENT CLUB
Real Madrid

JUDE BELLINGHAM

Jude Bellingham's talent was evident when he was just 16 years old! Now he has fulfilled that promise and become one of the world's best midfielders playing for one of the world's best clubs. He is a good tackler, exceptionally quick, positionally aware, and able to create and score goals.

DATE OF BIRTH	29/06/2003
POSITION	CENTRAL
HEIGHT	1.86 M
PRO DEBUT	2019
PREFERRED FOOT	RIGHT

 ASSISTS 44

 APPEARANCES 201

 DRIBBLES 600

 PASSES 9,408

 PENALTIES SCORED 3

SUCCESSFUL PASSES 86.1%

 GOALS 55

 SHOTS 354

 CHANCES CREATED 252

 TACKLES 387

MAJOR CLUB HONOURS
- ⚽ La Liga: 2024
- ⚽ UEFA Champions League: 2024
- ⚽ Bundesliga: runner-up 2023 (Borussia Dortmund)
- ⚽ DFB-Pokal: 2021 (Borussia Dortmund)

INTERNATIONAL HONOURS
- ⚽ UEFA European Championship: runner-up 2020 (2021), runner-up 2024

ACTIVITY AREAS

KEVIN DE BRUYNE

Kevin De Bruyne ranks as one of the finest attacking midfielders of his generation. Strong and technically brilliant, he can break up play at one end and almost immediately blast a 25-metre shot into the opposite goal. In 2025, he joined Napoli after a decade at Man City.

NATIONALITY Belgium

CURRENT CLUB Napoli

11

DATE OF BIRTH	28/06/1991
POSITION	ATTACKING
HEIGHT	1.81 M
PRO DEBUT	2008
PREFERRED FOOT	RIGHT

- APPEARANCES: 463
- ASSISTS: 184
- DRIBBLES: 1,287
- PASSES: 21,863
- SUCCESSFUL PASSES: 80.7%
- PENALTIES SCORED: 5
- GOALS: 116
- SHOTS: 1,105
- CHANCES CREATED: 1,314
- TACKLES: 531

MAJOR CLUB HONOURS
⚽ Premier League: 2018, 2019, 2021, 2022, 2023, 2024 (all Man City) ⚽ UEFA Champions League: runner-up 2021, 2023 (all Man City) ⚽ FA Cup: 2019, 2023 (all Man City) ⚽ DFB-Pokal: 2015 (VfL Wolfsburg)

INTERNATIONAL HONOURS
⚽ FIFA World Cup: third place 2018

ACTIVITY AREAS

23

NATIONALITY
Germany

CURRENT CLUB
Borussia Dortmund

EMRE CAN

Having been a defender earlier in his career, Emre Can has grown into a classy central midfielder. He combines his excellent tackling strength with his midfielder's instincts to thread passes to team-mates in attacking positions.

DATE OF BIRTH	12/01/1994
POSITION	CENTRAL
HEIGHT	1.86 M
PRO DEBUT	2011
PREFERRED FOOT	RIGHT

- ASSISTS: 21
- APPEARANCES: 412
- DRIBBLES: 650
- PENALTIES SCORED: 12
- PASSES: 20,910
- SUCCESSFUL PASSES: 85.6%
- GOALS: 37
- SHOTS: 341
- CHANCES CREATED: 244
- TACKLES: 880

MAJOR CLUB HONOURS
- Bundesliga: 2013 (B. Munich), runner-up 2023
- UEFA Champions League: 2013 (B. Munich), runner-up 2018 (Liverpool), runner-up 2024
- UEFA Europa League: runner-up 2016 (Liverpool)
- Serie A: 2019, 2020 (Juventus)
- DFB-Pokal: 2013 (B. Munich) 2021

INTERNATIONAL HONOURS
- FIFA Confederations Cup: 2017

ACTIVITY AREAS

EDUARDO CAMAVINGA

Eduardo Camavinga is outstanding as a defensive midfielder and also very effective at left-back. He reads the game extremely well, making timely interceptions and strong tackles and launching incisive attacks with his accurate passing. He has great stamina too.

NATIONALITY France

CURRENT CLUB Real Madrid

6

DATE OF BIRTH	10/11/2002
POSITION	DEFENSIVE
HEIGHT	1.85 M
PRO DEBUT	2019
PREFERRED FOOT	LEFT

- APPEARANCES: 234
- ASSISTS: 13
- DRIBBLES: 348
- PASSES: 8,741
- SUCCESSFUL PASSES: 89.8%
- PENALTIES SCORED: 0
- GOALS: 5
- SHOTS: 123
- CHANCES CREATED: 128
- TACKLES: 576

MAJOR CLUB HONOURS

⚽ La Liga: 2022, 2024 ⚽ UEFA Champions League: 2022, 2024 ⚽ Copa del Rey: 2023 ⚽ FIFA Club World Cup: 2022 ⚽ FIFA Intercontinental Cup: 2024

INTERNATIONAL HONOURS

⚽ FIFA World Cup: runner-up 2022

ACTIVITY AREAS

ALPHONSO DAVIES

NATIONALITY Canada
CURRENT CLUB Bayern Munich

19

Ghana-born Alphonso Davies is already considered one of the finest male footballers to represent Canada. He can confidently deliver in all left-sided positions thanks to his pace, dribbling talent, passing creativity, stamina and crossing ability.

DATE OF BIRTH	02/11/2000
POSITION	LEFT WING
HEIGHT	1.83 M
PRO DEBUT	2016
PREFERRED FOOT	LEFT

- ASSISTS: 38
- APPEARANCES: 270
- DRIBBLES: 1,226
- PENALTIES SCORED: 0
- PASSES: 11,332
- SUCCESSFUL PASSES: 86.9%
- GOALS: 20
- SHOTS: 180
- CHANCES CREATED: 306
- TACKLES: 463

MAJOR CLUB HONOURS
⚽ Bundesliga: 2019, 2020, 2021, 2022, 2023, 2025 ⚽ UEFA Champions League: 2020 ⚽ FIFA Club World Cup 2020 ⚽ UEFA Super Cup: 2020 ⚽ DFB-Pokal: 2019, 2020

INTERNATIONAL HONOURS
⚽ None to date

ACTIVITY AREAS

OUSMANE DEMBÉLÉ

Ousmane Dembélé's speed, dribbling skills and ability to take on defenders make him a natural winger. Capable of playing on either flank, he frequently uses his pace and technical skills to create goal-scoring opportunities for himself or provide key passes and assists to his team-mates.

NATIONALITY
France

CURRENT CLUB
Paris Saint-Germain

10

DATE OF BIRTH	15/05/1997
POSITION	WINGER
HEIGHT	1.78 M
PRO DEBUT	2014
PREFERRED FOOT	BOTH

- APPEARANCES 312
- ASSISTS 83
- DRIBBLES 1,498
- PASSES 9,507
- SUCCESSFUL PASSES 80%
- PENALTIES SCORED 3
- GOALS 86
- SHOTS 650
- CHANCES CREATED 565
- TACKLES 226

MAJOR CLUB HONOURS
⚽ Ligue 1: 2024, 2025 ⚽ UEFA Champions League: 2025 ⚽ La Liga: 2018, 2019, 2023 (all Barcelona) ⚽ Coupe de France: 2024, 2025 ⚽ FIFA World Club Cup: runner-up 2025 ⚽ Copa del Rey: 2018, 2021 (all Barcelona) ⚽ DFB Pokal: 2017 (Borussia Dortmund)

INTERNATIONAL HONOURS
⚽ FIFA World Cup: 2018, runner-up 2022
⚽ UEFA Nations League third place: 2025

ACTIVITY AREAS

NATIONALITY Portugal

CURRENT CLUB Manchester United

BRUNO FERNANDES

Bruno Fernandes shines as a central or attacking midfielder, but is comfortable playing in a defensive mode too. He has a fantastic eye for creating chances with through balls, driving powerful shots from long range, and is a master at converting penalties and free kicks.

DATE OF BIRTH	08/09/1994
POSITION	ATTACKING
HEIGHT	1.79 M
PRO DEBUT	2012
PREFERRED FOOT	RIGHT

- ASSISTS 92
- APPEARANCES 396
- DRIBBLES 684
- PASSES 17,939
- SUCCESSFUL PASSES 77.9%
- PENALTIES SCORED 38
- GOALS 111
- SHOTS 989
- CHANCES CREATED 907
- TACKLES 645

*Excludes data from Portuguese Premeira League

MAJOR CLUB HONOURS
⚽ UEFA Europa League: runner-up 2021, runner-up 2025 ⚽ Taça de Portugal: 2019 (Sporting CP) ⚽ Taça de Liga: 2018, 2019 (Sporting CP) ⚽ FA Cup: runner-up 2023, 2024

INTERNATIONAL HONOURS
⚽ UEFA Nations League: 2019, 2025

ACTIVITY AREAS

ENZO FERNÁNDEZ

The Argentinian has enjoyed a meteoric rise, most notably picking up the FIFA Best Young Player award at the 2022 World Cup. Playing in central midfield, he is happy to help his defenders, while his exceptionally accurate long-range passing often launches dangerous attacks.

NATIONALITY Argentina

CURRENT CLUB Chelsea

DATE OF BIRTH	17/01/2001
POSITION	CENTRAL
HEIGHT	1.78 M
PRO DEBUT	2019
PREFERRED FOOT	RIGHT

- APPEARANCES 97*
- ASSISTS 18
- DRIBBLES 141
- PENALTIES SCORED 1
- GOALS 11
- SHOTS 144
- TACKLES 193
- CHANCES CREATED 146
- PASSES 5,846
- SUCCESSFUL PASSES 86.8%

*Excludes data from Argentinian and Portuguese Leagues

MAJOR CLUB HONOURS
⚽ UEFA Conference League: 2025 ⚽ EFL Cup: 2025 ⚽ FIFA World Club Cup: 2025 ⚽ Argentina Primera División: 2021 (River Plate)

INTERNATIONAL HONOURS
⚽ FIFA World Cup: 2022
⚽ Copa América: 2024

ACTIVITY AREAS

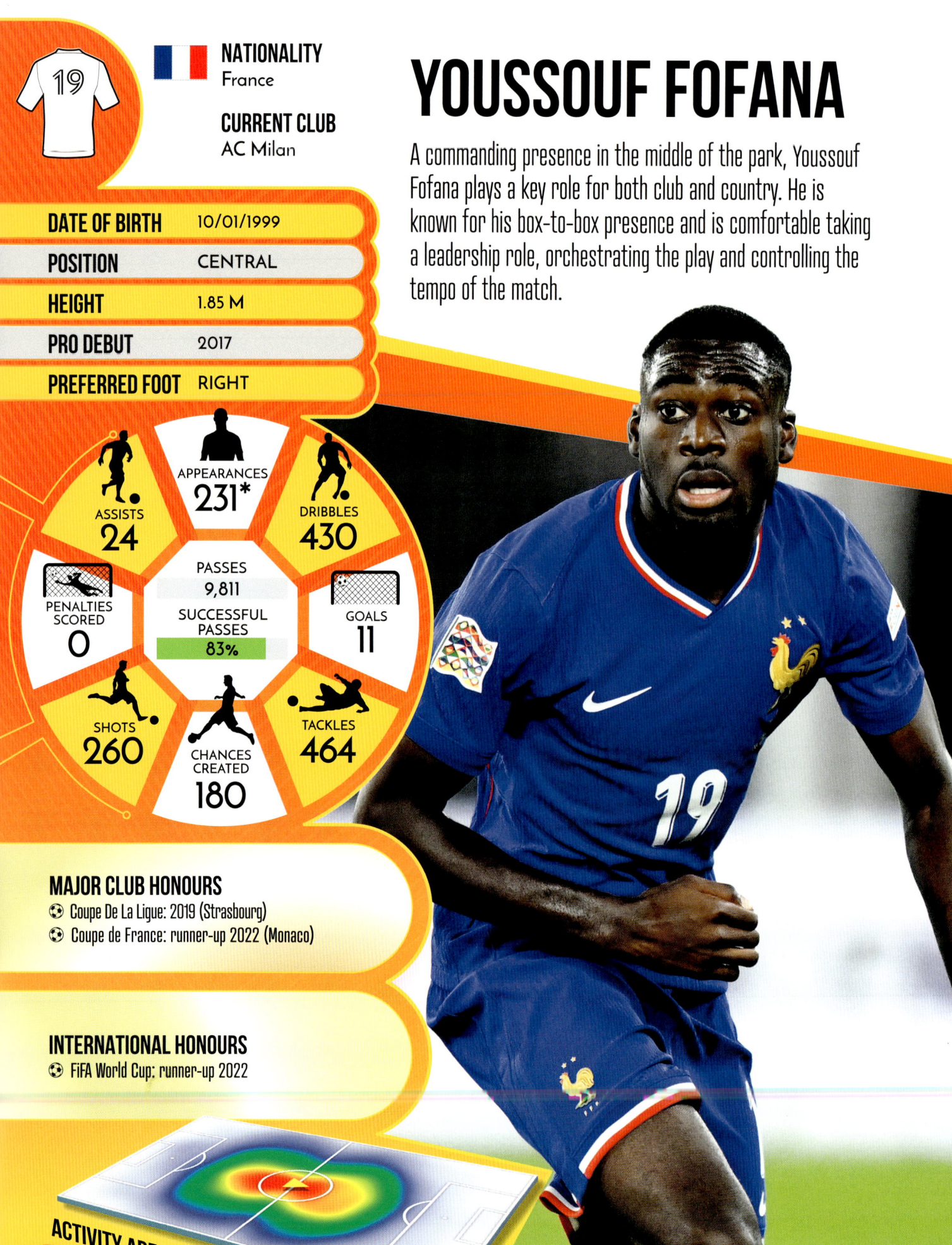

YOUSSOUF FOFANA

NATIONALITY: France
CURRENT CLUB: AC Milan

A commanding presence in the middle of the park, Youssouf Fofana plays a key role for both club and country. He is known for his box-to-box presence and is comfortable taking a leadership role, orchestrating the play and controlling the tempo of the match.

DATE OF BIRTH	10/01/1999
POSITION	CENTRAL
HEIGHT	1.85 M
PRO DEBUT	2017
PREFERRED FOOT	RIGHT

- ASSISTS: 24
- APPEARANCES: 231*
- DRIBBLES: 430
- PENALTIES SCORED: 0
- PASSES: 9,811
- SUCCESSFUL PASSES: 83%
- GOALS: 11
- SHOTS: 260
- CHANCES CREATED: 180
- TACKLES: 464

MAJOR CLUB HONOURS
- Coupe De La Ligue: 2019 (Strasbourg)
- Coupe de France: runner-up 2022 (Monaco)

INTERNATIONAL HONOURS
- FIFA World Cup: runner-up 2022

ACTIVITY AREAS

İLKAY GÜNDOĞAN

Although İlkay Gündoğan became a superstar quite late on in his career, his team-mates have always recognised his value. Admired for his solid defensive talent, great energy, passing ability and reading of the game, he often dictates the flow and tempo of a match.

NATIONALITY
Germany

CURRENT CLUB
Manchester City

22

DATE OF BIRTH	24/10/1990
POSITION	CENTRAL
HEIGHT	1.80 M
PRO DEBUT	2008
PREFERRED FOOT	RIGHT

- APPEARANCES: 522
- ASSISTS: 62
- DRIBBLES: 921
- PENALTIES SCORED: 5
- GOALS: 79
- SHOTS: 734
- CHANCES CREATED: 664
- TACKLES: 644
- PASSES: 29,002
- SUCCESSFUL PASSES: 89.4%

MAJOR CLUB HONOURS
- UEFA Champions League: 2023, runner-up 2021, runner-up 2013 (B. Dortmund)
- Premier League: 2018, 2019, 2021-23
- Bundesliga: 2012 (B. Dortmund)
- FA Cup: 2018, 2019, runner-up 2025
- DFB-Pokal: 2012 (B. Dortmund)

INTERNATIONAL HONOURS
- None to date

ACTIVITY AREAS

NATIONALITY
Netherlands

CURRENT CLUB
Barcelona

FRENKIE DE JONG

Frenkie de Jong has been an outstanding talent ever since he burst onto the scene as a teenager. His close control, work rate, passing accuracy and movement have seen him being compared to the great Johan Cruyff.

DATE OF BIRTH	12/05/1997
POSITION	CENTRAL
HEIGHT	1.80 M
PRO DEBUT	2015
PREFERRED FOOT	RIGHT

- ASSISTS: 18
- APPEARANCES: 244
- DRIBBLES: 372
- PENALTIES SCORED: 0
- PASSES: 14,865
- SUCCESSFUL PASSES: 92%
- GOALS: 15
- SHOTS: 89
- CHANCES CREATED: 248
- TACKLES: 319

MAJOR CLUB HONOURS
⚽ La Liga: 2023, 2025 ⚽ UEFA Europa League: runner-up 2017 (Ajax) ⚽ Copa del Rey: 2021, 2025 ⚽ Eredivisie: 2019 (Ajax) ⚽ KNVB Cup: 2019 (Ajax)

INTERNATIONAL HONOURS
⚽ UEFA Nations League: runner-up: 2019

ACTIVITY AREAS

JORGINHO

The talented Jorginho can control the tempo of play from deep, linking defence with midfield, and can even advance up the pitch and reach attackers with his accurate passing. He has the awareness, vision and passing ability to break lines, and can deliver lofted balls into the danger areas.

NATIONALITY
Italy

CURRENT CLUB
Arsenal

DATE OF BIRTH	20/12/1991
POSITION	DEFENSIVE
HEIGHT	1.80 M
PRO DEBUT	2010
PREFERRED FOOT	BOTH

- APPEARANCES: 425
- ASSISTS: 28
- DRIBBLES: 297
- PENALTIES SCORED: 35
- PASSES: 29,162
- SUCCESSFUL PASSES: 89.3%
- GOALS: 40
- SHOTS: 179
- CHANCES CREATED: 400
- TACKLES: 820

MAJOR CLUB HONOURS
- Premier League: runner-up 2023, runner-up 2024, runner-up 2025
- UEFA Champs League: 2021 (Chelsea)
- UEFA Europa League: 2019 (Chelsea)
- FIFA World Club Cup: 2021 (Chelsea)
- FA Cup: runner-up 2020-22 (Chelsea)
- Coppa Italia: 2014 (Napoli)

INTERNATIONAL HONOURS
- UEFA European Championship: 2020
- UEFA Nations League: third place 2021, third place 2023

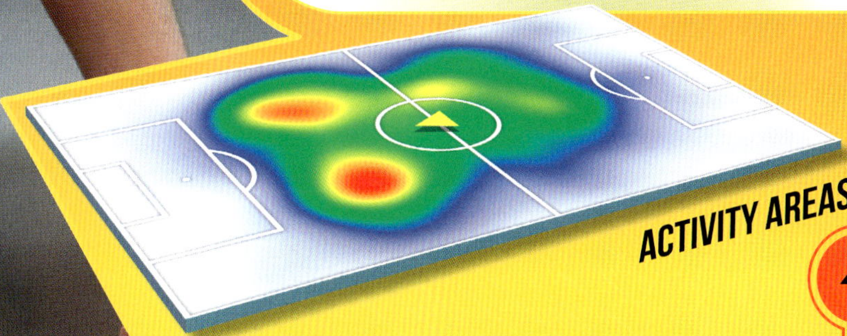

ACTIVITY AREAS

ALEXIS MAC ALLISTER

NATIONALITY Argentina
CURRENT CLUB Liverpool

Alexis Mac Allister is a versatile midfielder, equally efficient in central, attacking or defensive roles. He has great positional awareness, allowing him to break up attacks and then playing long, accurate downfield passes to team-mates in dangerous forward positions.

DATE OF BIRTH	24/12/1998
POSITION	CENTRAL
HEIGHT	1.76 M
PRO DEBUT	2016
PREFERRED FOOT	RIGHT

- ASSISTS 17
- APPEARANCES 180
- DRIBBLES 232
- PENALTIES SCORED 10
- PASSES 7,280
- SUCCESSFUL PASSES 86.5%
- GOALS 29
- SHOTS 272
- CHANCES CREATED 213
- TACKLES 391

MAJOR CLUB HONOURS
- Premier League: 2025
- EFL Cup: 2024, runner-up 2025

INTERNATIONAL HONOURS
- FIFA World Cup: 2022
- Copa América: 2024
- CONMEBOL–UEFA Cup of Champions: 2022

ACTIVITY AREAS

WESTON MCKENNIE

Tough and competitive on the pitch, Weston McKennie is a ball-winning midfielder with an instinct to break up play and interrupt the flow of the opposition. He likes making late runs into the box to join attacks, plus offers another weapon in attack — his extraordinarily long throws.

NATIONALITY USA

CURRENT CLUB Juventus

16

DATE OF BIRTH	28/08/1998
POSITION	CENTRAL
HEIGHT	1.85 M
PRO DEBUT	2017
PREFERRED FOOT	RIGHT

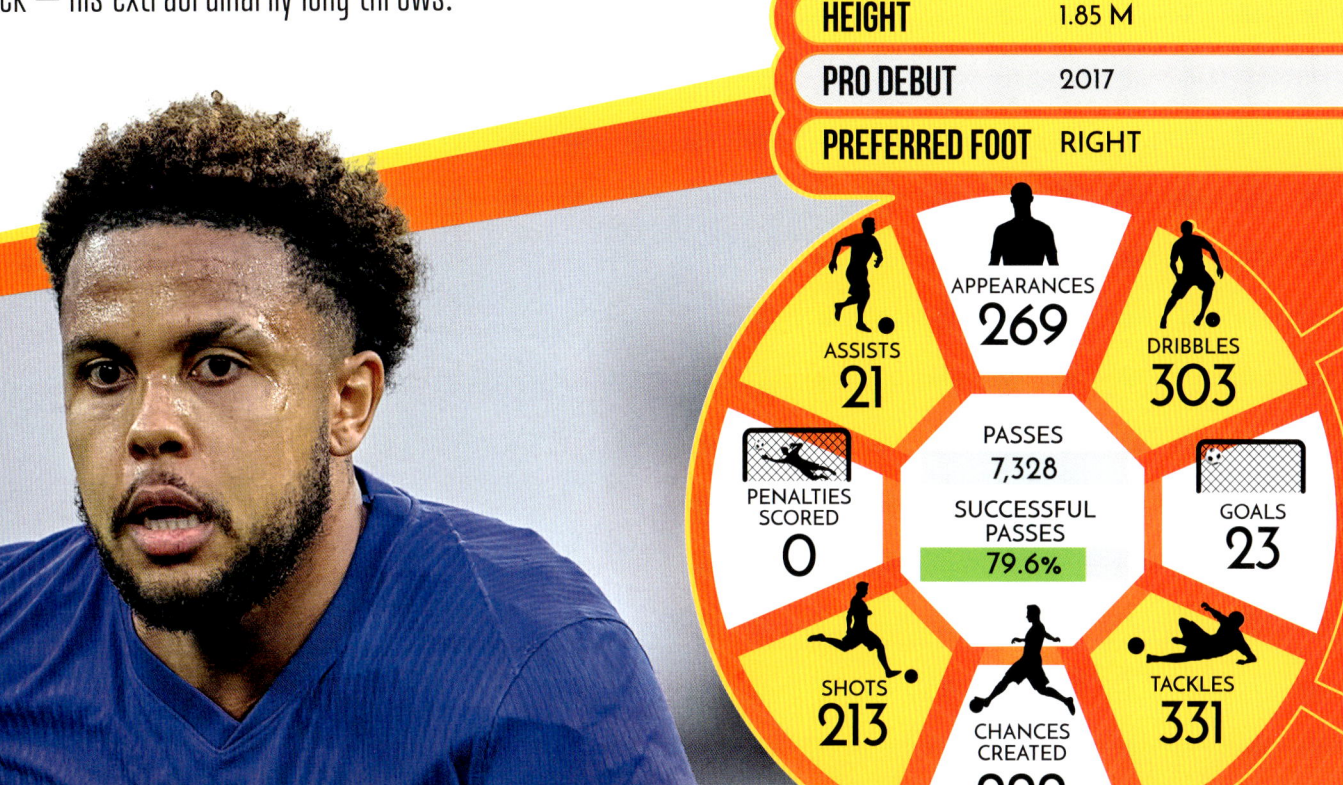

APPEARANCES 269
ASSISTS 21
DRIBBLES 303
PENALTIES SCORED 0
PASSES 7,328
SUCCESSFUL PASSES 79.6%
GOALS 23
SHOTS 213
CHANCES CREATED 222
TACKLES 331

MAJOR CLUB HONOURS
- Coppa Italia: 202, 2024

INTERNATIONAL HONOURS
- CONCACAF Nations League: 2020, 2023, 2024
- CONCACAF Gold Cup: runner-up: 2019

ACTIVITY AREAS

NATIONALITY
Croatia

CURRENT CLUB
AC Milan

LUKA MODRIĆ

A top player for more than 20 years (13 seasons with Real Madrid) and a Ballon d'Or winner in 2018, Luka Modrić is still capable of moments of magic on the pitch. He has a great footballing brain, can deliver long and short passes with both feet and can strike powerful long-range shots, especially free kicks.

DATE OF BIRTH	09/09/1985
POSITION	ATTACKING
HEIGHT	1.72 M
PRO DEBUT	2003
PREFERRED FOOT	RIGHT

- ASSISTS: 99
- APPEARANCES: 677
- DRIBBLES: 1513
- PENALTIES SCORED: 5
- PASSES: 37,487
- SUCCESSFUL PASSES: 89.2%
- GOALS: 53
- SHOTS: 765
- CHANCES CREATED: 1,057
- TACKLES: 842

MAJOR CLUB HONOURS

⚽ La Liga: 2017, 2020, 2022 (all Real Madrid) ⚽ UEFA Champions League: 2014, 2016, 2017, 2018, 2022, 2024 (all R. Mad.) ⚽ UEFA Super Cup: 2014, 2016, 2017, 2022 (all R. Mad.) ⚽ FIFA Club World Cup: 2014, 2016, 2017, 2018, 2022 (all R. Mad.) ⚽ Copa del Rey: 2014, 2023 (all R. Mad.)

INTERNATIONAL HONOURS

⚽ FIFA World Cup: runner-up 2018, third place 2022
⚽ UEFA Nations League: runner-up 2023

ACTIVITY AREAS

THOMAS MÜLLER

Thomas Müller is a dangerous attacking midfielder, who scores countless goals playing just behind a lone striker. The German powerhouse is mentally strong, tactically clever and great at finding holes in the opposition's defence. In 2025, he left Bayern Munich after 25 years with the club.

 **NATIONALITY** Germany

CURRENT CLUB TBC

DATE OF BIRTH	13/09/1989
POSITION	SECOND STRIKER
HEIGHT	1.85 M
PRO DEBUT	2008
PREFERRED FOOT	RIGHT

APPEARANCES 668
ASSISTS 198
DRIBBLES 1,072
PENALTIES SCORED 22
PASSES 20,852
SUCCESSFUL PASSES 76.9%
GOALS 207
SHOTS 1,245
CHANCES CREATED 1,222
TACKLES 664

MAJOR CLUB HONOURS
- Bundesliga: 2010, 2013, 2014, 2015, 2016, 2017, 2018, 2019, 2020, 2021, 2022, 2023, 2025 ⚽ DFB-Pokal: 2010, 2013, 2014, 2016, 2019, 2020 ⚽ UEFA Champions League: runner-up 2010, runner-up 2012, 2013, 2020 ⚽ FIFA Club World Cup: 2013, 2020

INTERNATIONAL HONOURS
- FIFA World Cup: 2014, third place 2010
- UEFA European Championship: third place 2012

ACTIVITY AREAS

JAMAL MUSIALA

Among the new generation of mega stars at Bayern, Jamal Musiala is a big-game player, famed for his exceptional pace and quick feet. Easy on the eye, he can dribble past defenders, find team-mates with inch-perfect passes and unleash powerful shots from any distance.

NATIONALITY Germany
CURRENT CLUB Bayern Munich

Shirt number: 25

DATE OF BIRTH	26/02/2003
POSITION	ATTACKING/WINGER
HEIGHT	1.84 M
PRO DEBUT	2020
PREFERRED FOOT	RIGHT

- ASSISTS 30
- APPEARANCES 185
- DRIBBLES 802
- PENALTIES SCORED 0
- PASSES 5,044
- SUCCESSFUL PASSES 84.4%
- GOALS 52
- SHOTS 336
- CHANCES CREATED 235
- TACKLES 226

MAJOR CLUB HONOURS
- Bundesliga: 2020, 2021, 2022, 2023, 2025
- UEFA Champions League: 2020
- FIFA Club World Cup: 2020

INTERNATIONAL HONOURS
- None to date

ACTIVITY AREAS

COLE PALMER

Although Cole Palmer is naturally left-footed, he is more than capable with his right, which makes him a strong dribbler who can unlock the tightest defences. Mentally strong and brimming with confidence, he strikes the ball sweetly, especially on penalties and free kicks.

 **NATIONALITY** England

CURRENT CLUB Chelsea

DATE OF BIRTH	06/05/2002
POSITION	ATTACKING
HEIGHT	1.85 M
PRO DEBUT	2020
PREFERRED FOOT	LEFT

- APPEARANCES 104
- ASSISTS 23
- DRIBBLES 258
- PENALTIES SCORED 13
- PASSES 3,192
- SUCCESSFUL PASSES 84%
- GOALS 39
- SHOTS 273
- CHANCES CREATED 177
- TACKLES 74

MAJOR CLUB HONOURS
⚽ Premier League: 2023 (Man. City) ⚽ UEFA Champions League: 2023 (Man. City) ⚽ FIFA World Club Cup: 2025 ⚽ UEFA Conference League: 2025 ⚽ FA Cup: 2023 (Man. City)

INTERNATIONAL HONOURS
⚽ UEFA European Championship: runner-up 2024

ACTIVITY AREAS

 11

NATIONALITY USA

CURRENT CLUB AC Milan

CHRISTIAN PULISIC

Although capable of playing in any attacking position, Christian Pulisic has recently been operating as a winger where he shows off his speed, strength and decision-making. He can run past defenders, inside or out, make dangerous runs into the penalty area and score goals.

DATE OF BIRTH	18/09/1998
POSITION	RIGHT
HEIGHT	1.77 M
PRO DEBUT	2016
PREFERRED FOOT	BOTH

ASSISTS 52
APPEARANCES 335
DRIBBLES 1253
PENALTIES SCORED 3
PASSES 7,686
SUCCESSFUL PASSES 81%
GOALS 70
SHOTS 485
CHANCES CREATED 365
TACKLES 311

MAJOR CLUB HONOURS
- UEFA Champions League: 2021 (Chelsea)
- UEFA Super Cup: 2021 (Chelsea)
- FIFA Club World Cup: 2021 (Chelsea)
- DFB-Pokal: 2017 (Borussia Dortmund)

INTERNATIONAL HONOURS
- CONCACAF Nations League: 2020, 2023, 2024
- ONCACAF Gold Cup: runner-up 2019

ACTIVITY AREAS

DECLAN RICE

Declan Rice has long been considered an exceptional defensive midfielder; now he has found an attacking flair playing in central midfield. He has added fine ball skills, passing, crossing and long-range shooting to his athleticism and tackling ability.

NATIONALITY England

CURRENT CURRENT CLUB Arsenal

41

DATE OF BIRTH	14/01/1999
POSITION	RIGHT
HEIGHT	1.87 M
PRO DEBUT	2017
PREFERRED FOOT	RIGHT

- ASSISTS 29
- APPEARANCES 321
- DRIBBLES 415
- PENALTIES SCORED 1
- PASSES 15,358
- SUCCESSFUL PASSES 88.7%
- GOALS 29
- SHOTS 296
- CHANCES CREATED 254
- TACKLES 681

MAJOR CLUB HONOURS
- Premier League: runner-up 2024, runner-up 2025
- UEFA Europa Conference League: 2023 (West Ham Utd)

INTERNATIONAL HONOURS
- UEFA European Championship: runner-up 2020 (2021), runner-up 2024
- UEFA Nations League: (third place) 2019

ACTIVITY AREAS

NATIONALITY England

CURRENT CLUB Arsenal

BUKAYO SAKA

A rising star in world football, Buyako Saka's versatility is just one of his talents. Equally good on both sides at full-back or wing-back, his creativity, positional sense, tackling, shooting and passing talents are displayed best as a right midfielder.

DATE OF BIRTH	05/09/2001
POSITION	WINGER
HEIGHT	1.78 M
PRO DEBUT	2018
PREFERRED FOOT	LEFT

 ASSISTS 59

 APPEARANCES 238

 DRIBBLES 752

 PENALTIES SCORED 12

PASSES 6,981
SUCCESSFUL PASSES 82%

 GOALS 68

 SHOTS 510

 CHANCES CREATED 413

 TACKLES 312

MAJOR CLUB HONOURS
⚽ Premier League: runner-up 2023, runner-up 2024, runner-up 2025 ⚽ FA Cup: 2020 ⚽ UEFA Europa League: runner-up 2019

INTERNATIONAL HONOURS
⚽ UEFA European Championship: runner-up 2020 (2021), runner-up 2024

ACTIVITY AREAS

LEROY SANÉ

Leroy Sané is almost the perfect example of a right-winger, except his left foot is stronger. He has all the other attributes to be fearsome on the flanks: great ball control, fine positional and tactical sense, top-class dribbling and outstanding pace to beat defenders.

NATIONALITY
Germany

CURRENT CLUB
Galatasaray (Turkey)

DATE OF BIRTH	11/01/1996
POSITION	WINGER
HEIGHT	1.83 M
PRO DEBUT	2014
PREFERRED FOOT	LEFT

- APPEARANCES 371
- ASSISTS 90
- DRIBBLES 1,651
- PASSES 10,317
- SUCCESSFUL PASSES 83.3%
- PENALTIES SCORED 0
- GOALS 100
- SHOTS 783
- CHANCES CREATED 510
- TACKLES 382

MAJOR CLUB HONOURS
⚽ Bundesliga: 2021, 2022, 2023, 2025 (all B. Munich) ⚽ FIFA Club World Cup: 2020 2021 (all B. Munich) ⚽ UEFA Super Cup: 2020 (B. Munich) ⚽ Premier League: 2018, 2019 (all Man. City) ⚽ FA Cup: 2019 (Man. City)

INTERNATIONAL HONOURS
⚽ FIFA Confederations Cup: 2017

ACTIVITY AREAS

AXEL WITSEL

NATIONALITY Belgium
CURRENT CLUB TBC

Originally a pacey right-winger, Axel Witsel has developed into a strong defensive presence in the middle of the park. He still has the ability to drive his team forward with both his play and leadership skills, as well as delivering dangerous passes with either foot.

DATE OF BIRTH	12/01/1989
POSITION	DEFENSIVE
HEIGHT	1.86 M
PRO DEBUT	2006
PREFERRED FOOT	RIGHT

- APPEARANCES: 296
- ASSISTS: 12
- DRIBBLES: 220
- PASSES: 15,897
- SUCCESSFUL PASSES: 91.9%
- PENALTIES SCORED: 1
- GOALS: 21
- SHOTS: 206
- CHANCES CREATED: 110
- TACKLES: 427

MAJOR CLUB HONOURS
- DFL-Pokal: 2021 (Borussia Dortmund)

INTERNATIONAL HONOURS
- FIFA World Cup: third place 2018

ACTIVITY AREAS

GRANIT XHAKA

Granit Xhaka makes any team he plays for much harder to break down with his performances in defensive midfield. One of the fittest players around, he combines boundless energy with great positional sense and fine tackling technique, and opponents must respect his long-range shooting ability.

NATIONALITY
Switzerland

CURRENT CLUB
Bayer Leverkusen

34

DATE OF BIRTH	27/09/1992
POSITION	DEFENSIVE
HEIGHT	1.86 M
PRO DEBUT	2010
PREFERRED FOOT	LEFT

- APPEARANCES 494
- ASSISTS 41
- DRIBBLES 489
- PENALTIES SCORED 1
- PASSES 34,461
- SUCCESSFUL PASSES 88.1%
- GOALS 34
- SHOTS 532
- CHANCES CREATED 502
- TACKLES 865

MAJOR CLUB HONOURS
⚽ Bundesliga: 2024 ⚽ UEFA Europa League: runner-up 2019 (Arsenal), runner-up 2024 ⚽ DFB-Pokal: 2024 ⚽ FA Cup: 2017, 2020 (Arsenal) ⚽ Swiss Super League: 2011, 2012 (all Basel)

INTERNATIONAL HONOURS
⚽ None to date

ACTIVITY AREAS

FORWARDS

The forwards are a team's frontline attackers and the chief goalscorers. They are also the team's most celebrated players. Whether it is the smaller, quicker player, such as Neymar and Mohamed Salah, or the bigger, more physical attacker, such as Erling Haaland and Romelu Lukaku, strikers have perfected the art of finding the back of the net on a regular basis. Aside from scoring lots of goals, the world's best strikers are also effective at creating chances for their team-mates.

WHAT DO THE STATS MEAN?

GOALS
This is the total number of goals a striker has scored. The figure spans across all the top clubs the player has represented so far in their career.

CONVERSION RATE
The percentage shows how good the player is at taking their chance in front of goal. If a player scores two goals from four shots, their conversion rate is 50 per cent

ASSISTS
A pass, cross or header to a team-mate who then scores counts as an assist. This stat also includes a deflected shot that is immediately converted by a team-mate.

MINUTES PER GOAL
This is the average length of time it takes for the player to score. It is calculated across all the minutes the player has played in their career at top level.

Did you know?

A perfect hat-trick is one where the player scores one goal with his right foot, another with his left foot and a third with his head. It does not matter in which order the goals come.

JONATHAN DAVID

NATIONALITY Canada
CURRENT CLUB Juventus

Jonathan David is a live wire on the pitch who combines speed, balance and excellent ball control. Normally used as second striker, feeding off a target man, he has a talent for finding holes in opposing defences, through which he can run or deliver inch-perfect passes.

DATE OF BIRTH	14/01/2000
POSITION	STRIKER
HEIGHT	1.78 M
PRO DEBUT	2018
PREFERRED FOOT	BOTH

- GOALS: 103
- PENALTIES SCORED: 24
- ASSISTS: 19
- APPEARANCES: 219
- SHOT CONVERSION: 22.2%
- MINUTES PER GOAL: 162
- GOALS LEFT: 33
- GOALS RIGHT: 63
- HAT-TRICKS: 3
- HEADED GOALS: 7
- SHOTS: 464

MAJOR CLUB HONOURS
- Ligue 1: 2021 (Lille)

INTERNATIONAL HONOURS
- None to date

ACTIVITY AREAS

MEMPHIS DEPAY

Memphis Depay is a striker who plays with intensity. He is an exceptional dribbler too and can play as a left-winger or left-sided striker. He is a brave player and will challenge the biggest defenders in the middle of the danger area.

NATIONALITY
Netherlands

CURRENT CLUB
Corinthians (Brazil)

DATE OF BIRTH	13/02/1994
POSITION	WINGER
HEIGHT	1.78 M
PRO DEBUT	2011
PREFERRED FOOT	RIGHT

- GOALS: 118
- PENALTIES SCORED: 20
- ASSISTS: 65
- GOALS RIGHT: 94
- SHOTS: 841
- HEADED GOALS: 5
- HAT-TRICKS: 3
- GOALS LEFT: 19
- APPEARANCES: 330
- SHOT CONVERSION: 14%
- MINUTES PER GOAL: 184

MAJOR CLUB HONOURS
⚽ La Liga: 2023 (Barcelona) ⚽ Eredivisie: 2015 (PSV Eindhoven) ⚽ KNVB Cup: 2012 (PSV Eindhoven) ⚽ Coupe de La Ligue: runner-up 2020 (Lyon)

INTERNATIONAL HONOURS
⚽ FIFA World Cup: third place 2014

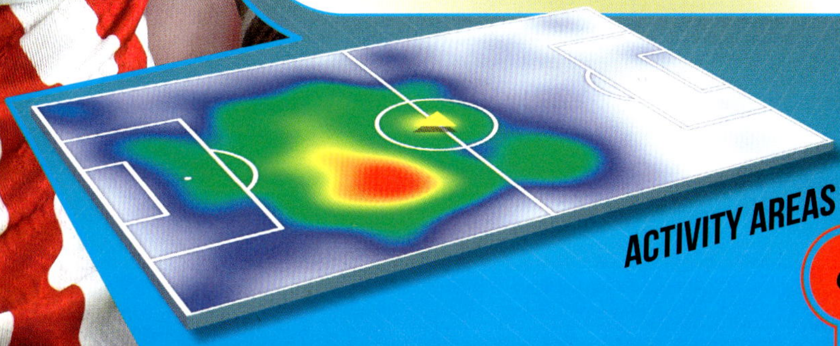

ACTIVITY AREAS

JOÃO FÉLIX

NATIONALITY Portugal
CURRENT CLUB Chelsea

Portugal's João Félix has developed into a technically gifted and intelligent goalscorer. Probably at his best as a second striker, linking with the midfield and making late runs into the box, he has good vision, control, dribbling skills and passing ability.

14

DATE OF BIRTH	10/11/1999
POSITION	FORWARD
HEIGHT	1.81 M
PRO DEBUT	2016
PREFERRED FOOT	RIGHT

- GOALS: 56
- PENALTIES SCORED: 4
- ASSISTS: 21
- APPEARANCES: 223
- SHOT CONVERSION: 12.3%
- MINUTES PER GOAL: 223
- GOALS LEFT: 9
- GOALS RIGHT: 42
- HAT-TRICKS: 1
- HEADED GOALS: 5
- SHOTS: 455

MAJOR CLUB HONOURS
- FIFA World Club Cup: 2025
- La Liga: 2021 (Atlético Madrid)
- Primeira Liga: 2019 (Benfica)

INTERNATIONAL HONOURS
- UEFA Nations League: 2019, 2025

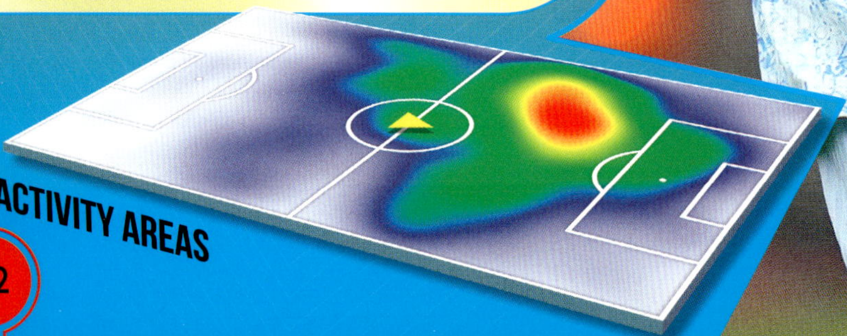

ACTIVITY AREAS

62

PHIL FODEN

Phil Foden can play in many positions: on either wing or centrally as a striker or playmaking midfielder. Naturally left-footed, he has an exceptional first touch, close control, poise, balance, tactical awareness, a powerful shot, pace and stamina. He can be a match winner on his day!

NATIONALITY England

CURRENT CLUB Manchester City

47

DATE OF BIRTH	28/05/2000
POSITION	SECOND STRIKER
HEIGHT	1.71 M
PRO DEBUT	2016
PREFERRED FOOT	LEFT

- GOALS: 79
- PENALTIES SCORED: 0
- ASSISTS: 40
- APPEARANCES: 254
- SHOT CONVERSION: 16%
- GOALS LEFT: 61
- MINUTES PER GOAL: 198
- GOALS RIGHT: 15
- HAT-TRICKS: 3
- HEADED GOALS: 3
- SHOTS: 495

MAJOR CLUB HONOURS
- Premier League: 2018, 2019, 2021, 2022, 2023, 2024
- UEFA Champions League: 2023, runners-up 2021
- UEFA Super Cup: 2023 FIFA Club World Cup: 2023
- FA Cup: 2019, 2023, runner-up 2024

INTERNATIONAL HONOURS
- UEFA European Championship: runner-up 2020, 2024

ACTIVITY AREAS

NATIONALITY
France

CURRENT CLUB
Los Angeles FC (USA)

OLIVIER GIROUD

Olivier Giroud is much more than a target man because his work-rate and positional sense make him hard to defend against near the goal. He uses his physique to hold and shield the ball, and is known for his accurate passing, shooting and heading.

DATE OF BIRTH	30/09/1986
POSITION	STRIKER
HEIGHT	1.93 M
PRO DEBUT	2005
PREFERRED FOOT	LEFT

- GOALS: 205
- PENALTIES SCORED: 23
- ASSISTS: 72
- APPEARANCES: 539
- SHOT CONVERSION: 15.9%
- MINUTES PER GOAL: 168
- GOALS LEFT: 123
- GOALS RIGHT: 20
- HAT-TRICKS: 7
- SHOTS: 1,292
- HEADED GOALS: 61

MAJOR CLUB HONOURS
- Serie A: 2022 (AC Milan) ⚽ UEFA Champions League: 2021 (Chelsea) ⚽ UEFA Europa League: 2019 (Chelsea) ⚽ Ligue 1: 2012 (Montpellier) ⚽ US Open Cup: 2024 ⚽ FA Cup: 2014, 2015, 2017 (all Arsenal), 2018 (Chelsea) 2017 (Arsenal), 2018 (Chelsea)

INTERNATIONAL HONOURS
- ⚽ FIFA World Cup 2018, runner-up 2022
- ⚽ UEFA European Championship: runner-up 2016

ACTIVITY AREAS

ANTOINE GRIEZMANN

NATIONALITY
France

Known for being the ultimate team player, Antoine Griezmann is able to take on all offensive roles, be it as a front man, attacking midfielder, false NO.9 or coming from wide positions. He is an excellent team-mate, using his experience to get the best out of everyone on the pitch.

CURRENT CLUB
Atlético Madrid

DATE OF BIRTH	21/03/1991
POSITION	STRIKER
HEIGHT	1.76 M
PRO DEBUT	2009
PREFERRED FOOT	LEFT

- GOALS: 246
- PENALTIES SCORED: 16
- ASSISTS: 102
- APPEARANCES: 644
- SHOT CONVERSION: 16.4%
- MINUTES PER GOAL: 200
- GOALS LEFT: 181
- GOALS RIGHT: 34
- HAT-TRICKS: 5
- HEADED GOALS: 31
- SHOTS: 1,501

MAJOR CLUB HONOURS
- UEFA Champions League: runner-up 2016
- UEFA Europa League 2018 ⚽ UEFA Super Cup 2018
- Copa del Rey 2021 (Barcelona)

INTERNATIONAL HONOURS
- FIFA World Cup: 2018, runner-up 2022
- UEFA European Championship: runner-up 2016
- UEFA Nations League: 2021

ACTIVITY AREAS

NATIONALITY Norway

CURRENT CLUB Manchester City

ERLING HAALAND

Erling Haaland terrorises defences with his blistering pace, aerial ability, strength, energy, timing and attacking instincts. He is tall, extremely fast, well-balanced, good with both feet, an excellent passer and a powerful shooter in open play or at set pieces.

DATE OF BIRTH	21/07/2000
POSITION	STRIKER
HEIGHT	1.94 M
PRO DEBUT	2015
PREFERRED FOOT	LEFT

- GOALS: 196
- PENALTIES SCORED: 33
- ASSISTS: 36
- APPEARANCES: 214
- SHOT CONVERSION: 26.4%
- MINUTES PER GOAL: 89
- GOALS LEFT: 142
- GOALS RIGHT: 29
- HAT-TRICKS: 13
- HEADED GOALS: 24
- SHOTS: 742

MAJOR CLUB HONOURS
⚽ Premier League: 2023, 2024 ⚽ UEFA Champions League: 2023 ⚽ DFB-Pokal: 2021 (Borussia Dortmund) ⚽ Austrian Bundesliga: 2019, 2020 (Red Bull Salzburg) ⚽ FA Cup: 2023, runner-up 2024, runner-up 2025 ⚽ Austrian Cup: 2019 (Red Bull Salzburg)

INTERNATIONAL HONOURS
⚽ None to date

ACTIVITY AREAS

ALEXANDER ISAK

Alexander Isak is a complete striker, scoring and setting up goals with both feet and his head. He displays speed of thought and movement, together with great positional sense and timing, as well as helping out in defence when necessary.

NATIONALITY Sweden

CURRENT CLUB Newcastle

14

DATE OF BIRTH	21/09/1999
POSITION	STRIKER
HEIGHT	1.92 M
PRO DEBUT	2016
PREFERRED FOOT	RIGHT

- GOALS: 91
- PENALTIES SCORED: 13
- ASSISTS: 14
- GOALS RIGHT: 66
- SHOTS: 472
- HEADED GOALS: 10
- HAT-TRICKS: 2
- GOALS LEFT: 15
- APPEARANCES: 219
- SHOT CONVERSION: 19.3%
- MINUTES PER GOAL: 155

MAJOR CLUB HONOURS
⚽ Football League Cup: 2025 ⚽ Copa del Rey 2020 (Real Sociedad) ⚽ DFB-Pokal: 2017 (Borussia Dortmund)

INTERNATIONAL HONOURS
⚽ None to date

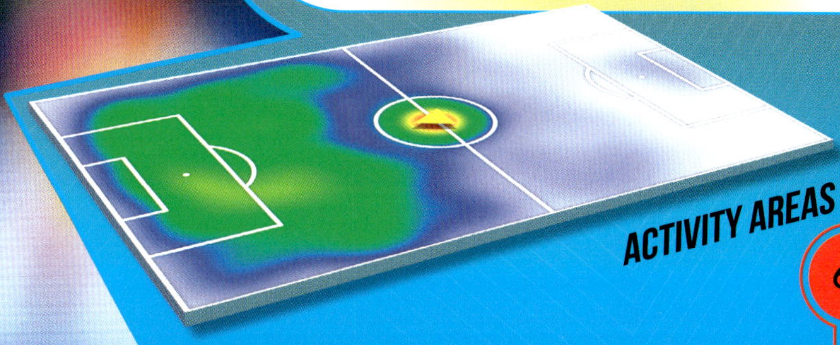

ACTIVITY AREAS

NATIONALITY
Serbia

CURRENT CLUB
TBC

LUKA JOVIĆ

Luka Jović is a predator in the penalty box. He uses his speed and attacking instincts to find spaces in the penalty area and score goals from close range with deft touches from either foot and occasionally his head. He left AC Milan at the end of the 2024/25 season.

DATE OF BIRTH	23/12/1997
POSITION	STRIKER
HEIGHT	1.81 M
PRO DEBUT	2014
PREFERRED FOOT	RIGHT

- GOALS: 63
- PENALTIES SCORED: 1
- APPEARANCES: 219
- ASSISTS: 15
- SHOT CONVERSION: 16.4%
- MINUTES PER GOAL: 159
- GOALS LEFT: 20
- GOALS RIGHT: 28
- HAT-TRICKS: 1
- HEADED GOALS: 15
- SHOTS: 384

MAJOR CLUB HONOURS
- La Liga: 2020, 2022 (Real Madrid)
- UEFA Champions League: 2022 (Real Madrid)
- UEFA Conference League: runner-up 2023 (Fiorentina)
- DFB-Pokal: 2018 (Eintracht Frankfurt)

INTERNATIONAL HONOURS
- None to date

ACTIVITY AREAS

68

HARRY KANE

Harry Kane has grown into the complete striker. His power in the air, skills with both feet and superb ball-striking technique make him hard to defend against. What's more, with his defence-splitting passes, he also sets up many goals for his team-mates.

 **NATIONALITY** England

CURRENT CLUB Bayern Munich

DATE OF BIRTH	28/07/1993
PInitialPOSITION	STRIKER
HEIGHT	1.88 M
PRO DEBUT	2009
PREFERRED FOOT	RIGHT

- GOALS: 330
- PENALTIES SCORED: 58
- ASSISTS: 79
- GOALS RIGHT: 203
- SHOTS: 1,729
- HEADED GOALS: 66
- HAT-TRICKS: 19
- GOALS LEFT: 59
- APPEARANCES: 475
- SHOT CONVERSION: 19.1%
- MINUTES PER GOAL: 118

MAJOR CLUB HONOURS
⚽ Bundesliga: 2025 ⚽ UEFA Champions League: runner-up 2019 (Tottenham Hotspur)

INTERNATIONAL HONOURS
⚽ UEFA European Championship: runner-up 2020 (2021), runner-up 2024 ⚽ UEFA Nations League: third place 2019

ACTIVITY AREAS

NATIONALITY Poland
CURRENT CLUB Barcelona

ROBERT LEWANDOWSKI

Robert Lewandowski has consistently ranked as one of the world's best strikers since he made his debut at Borussia Dortmund in 2010. His positioning, technique, power and finishing saw him net more than 300 goals in the Bundesliga before he made his move to Barcelona in 2022.

DATE OF BIRTH	21/08/1988
POSITION	STRIKER
HEIGHT	1.85 M
PRO DEBUT	2005
PREFERRED FOOT	RIGHT

- GOALS: 489
- PENALTIES SCORED: 67
- ASSISTS: 94
- APPEARANCES: 637
- SHOT CONVERSION: 20.6%
- MINUTES PER GOAL: 106
- GOALS LEFT: 84
- GOALS RIGHT: 323
- HAT-TRICKS: 24
- HEADED GOALS: 78
- SHOTS: 2,371

MAJOR CLUB HONOURS

⚽ La Liga: 2023, 2025 ⚽ Bundesliga: 2011, 2012 (all B. Dortmund), 2015, '16, '17, '18, '19, '20, '21, '22 (all B. Munich) ⚽ UEFA Champions League: 2020 (B. Munich) ⚽ FIFA Club World Cup: 2020 (B. Munich) ⚽ Copa del Rey: 2025

INTERNATIONAL HONOURS

⚽ None to date

ACTIVITY AREAS

ADEMOLA LOOKMAN

Ademola Lookman was raised in England, where he developed his skills, but it was in Italy that he achieved success in top-flight football. Creative, dynamic, direct and with electric pace, he has quick feet, great control, a powerful shot with either foot and is excellent in the air.

NATIONALITY
Nigeria

CURRENT CLUB
Atalanta

Shirt number: 11

DATE OF BIRTH	20/10/1997
POSITION	WINGER
HEIGHT	1.74 M
PRO DEBUT	2015
PREFERRED FOOT	BOTH

- GOALS: 67
- PENALTIES SCORED: 4
- ASSISTS: 34
- APPEARANCES: 249
- SHOT CONVERSION: 40.6%
- MINUTES PER GOAL: 214
- GOALS LEFT: 17
- GOALS RIGHT: 45
- HAT-TRICKS: 1
- HEADED GOALS: 5
- SHOTS: 165

MAJOR CLUB HONOURS
- UEFA Europe League: 2024

INTERNATIONAL HONOURS
- Africa Cup of Nations: runner-up 2023
- FIFA U-20 World Cup: 2017 (England)

ACTIVITY AREAS

NATIONALITY	Belgium
CURRENT CLUB	Napoli

ROMELU LUKAKU

Romelu Lukaku has a breathtaking pace and dribbling ability. Although he normally plays on the wing, he can also be dangerous in the middle of the park as he can leap high to win headers and shoot powerfully with either foot.

DATE OF BIRTH	13/05/1993
POSITION	STRIKER
HEIGHT	1.91 M
PRO DEBUT	2009
PREFERRED FOOT	LEFT

- GOALS: 251
- PENALTIES SCORED: 29
- ASSISTS: 78
- APPEARANCES: 532
- SHOT CONVERSION: 19.3%
- MINUTES PER GOAL: 159
- GOALS LEFT: 144
- GOALS RIGHT: 59
- HAT-TRICKS: 4
- HEADED GOALS: 44
- SHOTS: 1,298

MAJOR CLUB HONOURS
⚽ Serie A: 2021 (Inter Milan), 2025 ⚽ UEFA Champions League: runner-up 2023 (Inter Milan) ⚽ Coppa Italia: 2023 (Inter Milan) ⚽ FIFA Club World Cup: 2021 (Chelsea) ⚽ UEFA Europa League: runner-up 2020 (Chelsea)

INTERNATIONAL HONOURS
⚽ FIFA World Cup: third place 2018

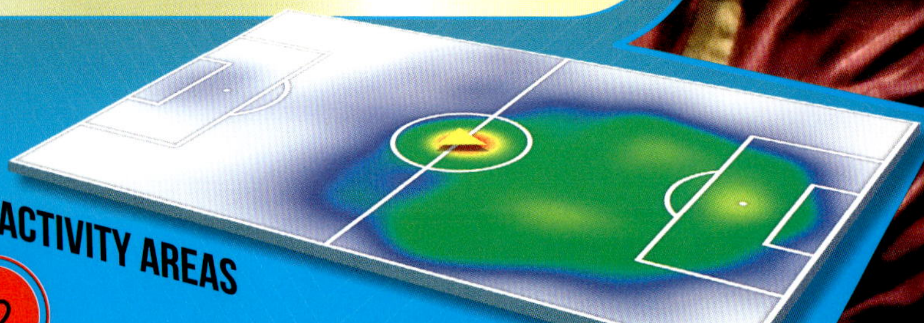

ACTIVITY AREAS

90

72

KYLIAN MBAPPÉ

A FIFA World Cup winner with France at just 18 and a runner-up four years later, Kylian Mbappé is counted among the best strikers in world football today. The pacey finisher is a superb ball player who consistently gets on the score sheet and sets up chances for his team-mates.

NATIONALITY France

CURRENT CLUB Real Madrid

DATE OF BIRTH	20/12/1998
POSITION	STRIKER
HEIGHT	1.78 M
PRO DEBUT	2015
PREFERRED FOOT	RIGHT

- GOALS: 278
- PENALTIES SCORED: 33
- ASSISTS: 93
- GOALS RIGHT: 217
- SHOTS: 1,322
- HEADED GOALS: 8
- HAT-TRICKS: 14
- GOALS LEFT: 53
- APPEARANCES: 369
- SHOT CONVERSION: 21%
- MINUTES PER GOAL: 102

MAJOR CLUB HONOURS

⚽ Ligue 1: 2017 (Monaco), 2018, 2019, 2020, 2022, 2023, 2024 (all PSG) ⚽ UEFA Champions League: runner-up 2020 (PSG) ⚽ Coupe de France: 2018, 2020, 2021, 2024 (all PSG) ⚽ FIFA Intercontinental Cup: 2024

INTERNATIONAL HONOURS

⚽ FIFA World Cup: 2018, runner-up 2022
⚽ UEFA Nations League: 2021

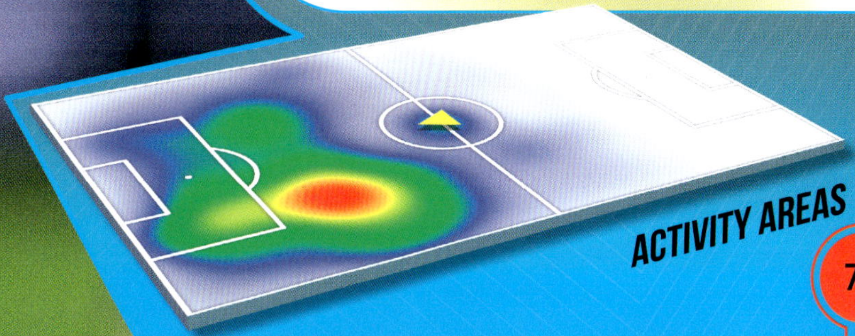

ACTIVITY AREAS

LIONEL MESSI

NATIONALITY Argentina
CURRENT CLUB Inter Miami (USA)

The greatest player of his generation, if not the greatest ever, the 2022 World Cup winner is a fine playmaker with a stunning goal-scoring record. He is also a fantastically fast dribbler who can carve out opportunities to shoot with either foot, from any range and rarely misses the target.

DATE OF BIRTH	24/06/1987
POSITION	FORWARD
HEIGHT	1.70 M
PRO DEBUT	2003
PREFERRED FOOT	LEFT

- GOALS: 659
- PENALTIES SCORED: 79
- APPEARANCES: 778
- ASSISTS: 281
- SHOT CONVERSION: 18.8%
- MINUTES PER GOAL: 98
- GOALS LEFT: 548
- GOALS RIGHT: 87
- HAT-TRICKS: 45
- HEADED GOALS: 22
- SHOTS: 3,504

MAJOR CLUB HONOURS
- Ligue 1: 2022, 2023 (PSG)
- La Liga: 2005, '06, '09, '10, '11, '13, '15, '16, '18, '19 (all Barça)
- UEFA Champions League: 2006, '09, '11, '15 (all Barça)
- UEFA Super Cup: 2009, '11, '15 (all Barça)
- FIFA Club World Cup: 2009, '11, '15 (all Barça)
- MLS Leagues Cup: 2023

INTERNATIONAL HONOURS
- FIFA World Cup: 2022, runner-up 2014
- Olympic Games: gold medal 2008
- Copa América: 2021, 2024, runner-up* 2007*, 2015*, 2016*

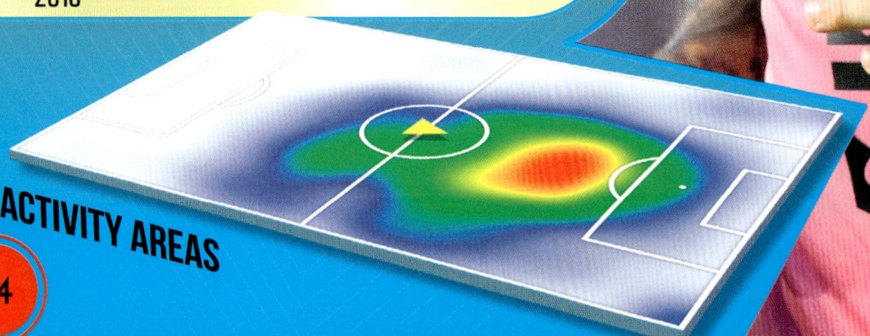

ACTIVITY AREAS

ÁLVARO MORATA

Álvaro Morata is perfectly built for a central striker. Tall, strong and excellent in the air, he is comfortable with the ball at his feet. Morata is also surprisingly fast and has great tactical and positional awareness.

NATIONALITY Spain

CURRENT CLUB AC Milan

DATE OF BIRTH	23/10/1992
POSITION	STRIKER
HEIGHT	1.90 M
PRO DEBUT	2010
PREFERRED FOOT	RIGHT

- GOALS: 164
- PENALTIES SCORED: 7
- ASSISTS: 57
- APPEARANCES: 480
- SHOT CONVERSION: 18%
- MINUTES PER GOAL: 162
- GOALS LEFT: 40
- GOALS RIGHT: 83
- HAT-TRICKS: 3
- HEADED GOALS: 41
- SHOTS: 913

MAJOR CLUB HONOURS
- La Liga: 2012, 2017 (R. Madrid)
- Serie A: 2015, 2016 (all Juventus)
- UEFA Champions League: 2014, '17 (R. Madrid), runner-up 2015 (Juventus)
- UEFA Europa League: 2019 (Chelsea)
- UEFA Super Cup: 2016 (R. Madrid)
- FIFA Club World Cup: 2016 (R. Madrid)

INTERNATIONAL HONOURS
- UEFA European Championship: 2024
- UEFA Nations League: 2023, runner-up 2025
- UEFA European U-21 Championship: 2013

ACTIVITY AREAS

NATIONALITY
Brazil

CURRENT CLUB
Santos (Brazil)

NEYMAR

Neymar's outstanding football career has gone full circle and he is back where it all began at Santos in Brazil. He still possesses the pace and phenomenal dribbling to beat defenders in numbers, and can strike fear into the opposition defence with his playmaking skills.

DATE OF BIRTH	05/02/1992
POSITION	FORWARD
HEIGHT	1.75 M
PRO DEBUT	2009
PREFERRED FOOT	RIGHT

- GOALS: 228
- PENALTIES SCORED: 40
- APPEARANCES: 390
- ASSISTS: 128
- SHOT CONVERSION: 19.8%
- MINUTES PER GOAL: 138
- GOALS LEFT: 53
- GOALS RIGHT: 153
- HAT-TRICKS: 10
- HEADED GOALS: 8
- SHOTS: 1,152

MAJOR CLUB HONOURS
⚽ La Liga: 2015, '16, '17 (all Barça) ⚽ Ligue 1: 2018, '19 '20, 2022, 2023 (all PSG) ⚽ UEFA Champions League: 2016 (Barça), runner-up 2020 (PSG) ⚽ FIFA Club World Cup: 2016 (Barça) ⚽ Copa del Rey: 2015, '16, '17 (all Barça) ⚽ Coupe de France: 2018, '20, '21 (all PSG)

INTERNATIONAL HONOURS
⚽ Copa América: runner-up 2021
⚽ FIFA Confederations Cup: 2013
⚽ Olympic Games: silver medal 2012, gold medal 2016

ACTIVITY AREAS

MARCUS RASHFORD

A great player to watch when he is on form, Marcus Rashford has scored some stunning goals for both club and country. He prefers to raid from the left side, to be on his stronger right foot, but his pace and heading ability make him just as dangerous in the middle.

NATIONALITY England

CURRENT CLUB Barcelona (on loan)

DATE OF BIRTH	31/10/1997
POSITION	FORWARD
HEIGHT	1.80 M
PRO DEBUT	2015
PREFERRED FOOT	RIGHT

- GOALS: 115
- PENALTIES SCORED: 11
- ASSISTS: 51
- GOALS RIGHT: 91
- SHOTS: 803
- HEADED GOALS: 9
- HAT-TRICKS: 1
- GOALS LEFT: 15
- APPEARANCES: 377
- SHOT CONVERSION: 14.3%
- MINUTES PER GOAL: 219

MAJOR CLUB HONOURS
- UEFA Europa League: 2017, runner-up 2021 (all Man. United)
- FA Cup: 2016, runner-up 2023, 2024 (all Man. United)
- FA Cup 2016, 2024 (Man. United)

INTERNATIONAL HONOURS
- UEFA European Championship: runner-up 2020 (2021)
- UEFA Nations League: third place 2019

ACTIVITY AREAS

| NATIONALITY | Portugal |
| CURRENT CLUB | Al Nassr (S. Arabia) |

CRISTIANO RONALDO

The superstar striker has wowed fans across the world with his all-around attacking skills. He is breathtaking to watch when he is running at defenses, brilliant in the air, and a superb finisher with an extraordinary goal-scoring record.

DATE OF BIRTH	05/02/1985
POSITION	FORWARD
HEIGHT	1.88 M
PRO DEBUT	2002
PREFERRED FOOT	RIGHT

- GOALS: 704
- PENALTIES SCORED: 139
- APPEARANCES: 820
- ASSISTS: 189
- SHOT CONVERSION: 14.8%
- MINUTES PER GOAL: 99
- GOALS LEFT: 121
- GOALS RIGHT: 470
- HAT-TRICKS: 53
- HEADED GOALS: 111
- SHOTS: 4,743

MAJOR CLUB HONOURS

⚽ UEFA Champions League: 2008 (Man. U), 2014, '16, '17, '18 (R. Madrid) ⚽ FIFA Club World Cup: 2008 (Man. U), 2014, '16, '17 (R. Madrid) ⚽ UEFA Super Cup: 2014, '17 (R. Madrid) ⚽ Serie A: 2019, '20 (Juventus) ⚽ Premier League: 2007, '08, '09 (Man. U) ⚽ La Liga: 2012, '17 (R. Madrid)

INTERNATIONAL HONOURS

⚽ UEFA European Championship: 2016
⚽ UEFA Nations League: 2019, 2025

ACTIVITY AREAS

MOHAMED SALAH

The two-time African Footballer Of The Year is a brilliant left-footed attacker who prowls the left wing. Mo Salah has amazing pace with the ability to make angled runs, finding gaps in defences before scoring spectacular goals.

NATIONALITY Egypt

CURRENT CLUB Liverpool

DATE OF BIRTH	15/06/1992
POSITION	WINGER
HEIGHT	1.75 M
PRO DEBUT	2010
PREFERRED FOOT	LEFT

- GOALS: 278
- PENALTIES SCORED: 42
- ASSISTS: 132
- GOALS RIGHT: 41
- SHOTS: 1,620
- HEADED GOALS: 10
- HAT-TRICKS: 6
- GOALS LEFT: 227
- APPEARANCES: 508
- SHOT CONVERSION: 17.2%
- MINUTES PER GOAL: 145

MAJOR CLUB HONOURS

⚽ Premier League: 2020, 2025 ⚽ UEFA Champions League: 2019, runner-up 2018, runner-up 2022 ⚽ UEFA Super Cup: 2019 ⚽ FIFA Club World Cup: 2019 ⚽ FA Cup: 2022

INTERNATIONAL HONOURS

⚽ CAF Africa Cup of Nations: runner-up 2017, runner-up 2021

ACTIVITY AREAS

SON HEUNG-MIN

NATIONALITY South Korea
CURRENT CLUB Tottenham Hotspur

Son Heung-Min is at his best when he plays behind the main striker. Although excellent with both feet, attacking from the right side is his strength and he converts a lot of chances that are set up by knock-downs or passes across the box.

DATE OF BIRTH	08/07/1992
POSITION	WINGER
HEIGHT	1.84 M
PRO DEBUT	2010
PREFERRED FOOT	BOTH

- GOALS 197
- PENALTIES SCORED 5
- ASSISTS 90
- GOALS RIGHT 111
- SHOTS 1,198
- HEADED GOALS 10
- HAT-TRICKS 6
- GOALS LEFT 76
- APPEARANCES 552
- SHOT CONVERSION 16.4%
- MINUTES PER GOAL 198

MAJOR CLUB HONOURS
- UEFA Champions League: runner-up 2019
- UEFA Europa League: 2025

INTERNATIONAL HONOURS
- AFC Asian Cup: runner-up 2015

ACTIVITY AREAS

VINÍCIUS JÚNIOR

Vinícius Júnior loves terrorising right-backs, attacking off the left flank, cutting inside to deliver crosses or shooting with his favoured right foot. He brings flair and panache, combined with blistering pace and fantastic dribbling, making him truly world class on his day.

NATIONALITY Brazil
CURRENT CLUB Real Madrid

DATE OF BIRTH	12/07/2000
POSITION	WINGER
HEIGHT	1.76 M
PRO DEBUT	2017
PREFERRED FOOT	RIGHT

- GOALS: 97
- PENALTIES SCORED: 5
- ASSISTS: 63
- APPEARANCES: 313
- SHOT CONVERSION: 14.5%
- MINUTES PER GOAL: 216
- GOALS LEFT: 19
- GOALS RIGHT: 71
- HAT-TRICKS: 3
- HEADED GOALS: 5
- SHOTS: 668

MAJOR CLUB HONOURS
⚽ La Liga: 2020, 2022, 2024 ⚽ UEFA Champions League: 2022, 2024 ⚽ FIFA Club World Cup: 2018, 2022 ⚽ UEFA Super Cup: 2022 ⚽ Copa del Rey: 2023 ⚽ FIFA Intercontinental Cup: 2024

INTERNATIONAL HONOURS
⚽ None to date

ACTIVITY AREAS

NICO WILLIAMS

NATIONALITY Spain
CURRENT CLUB Atlético Madrid

Nico Williams is yet another footballer to come off Spain's production line of talent. Mainly a left-winger, he uses his sublime pace to get past defenders and deliver dangerous crosses, often setting up chances for his older brother Iñaki at Atlético Madrid.

DATE OF BIRTH	12/07/2002
POSITION	LEFT-WINGER
HEIGHT	1.81 M
PRO DEBUT	2020
PREFERRED FOOT	RIGHT

- GOALS: 21
- PENALTIES SCORED: 0
- ASSISTS: 22
- APPEARANCES: 145
- SHOT CONVERSION: 9%
- MINUTES PER GOAL: 442
- GOALS LEFT: 8
- GOALS RIGHT: 11
- HAT-TRICKS: 0
- HEADED GOALS: 2
- SHOTS: 233

MAJOR CLUB HONOURS
- Copa del Rey: 2024

INTERNATIONAL HONOURS
- UEFA European Championship: 2024
- UEFA Nations League: runner-up 2025

ACTIVITY AREAS

LAMINE YAMAL

Regarded as a prodigy of the modern game, Lamine Yamal is technically gifted, especially with his favoured left foot, curling crosses towards the goal. He also plays as a central striker or attacking midfielder, using his pace and control to beat defenders and set up dangerous attacks.

 **NATIONALITY** Spain

CURRENT CLUB Barcelona

 19

DATE OF BIRTH	13/07/2007
POSITION	RIGHT-WINGER
HEIGHT	1.80 M
PRO DEBUT	2023
PREFERRED FOOT	LEFT

- GOALS: 19
- PENALTIES SCORED: 0
- ASSISTS: 23
- APPEARANCES: 96
- SHOT CONVERSION: 6.9%
- MINUTES PER GOAL: 355
- GOALS LEFT: 17
- GOALS RIGHT: 2
- HAT-TRICKS: 0
- HEADED GOALS: 0
- SHOTS: 277

MAJOR CLUB HONOURS
⚽ La Liga 2023, 2025 ⚽ Copa del Rey: 2025

INTERNATIONAL HONOURS
⚽ UEFA European Championship: 2024 ⚽ UEFA Nations League: runner-up 2024

ACTIVITY AREAS

GOALKEEPERS

The goalkeeper is a team's last line of defence and, unlike the other positions, there is no one playing next to them. There is more pressure on goalkeepers than in any other position because when a keeper makes an error, the chances are that the other team will score. The goalies featured in this section are all great shot-stoppers, but some play outside their penalty areas as sweeper-keepers; others have made their reputation as penalty-savers; then there are those who are great at catching the ball or punching it clear.

WHAT DO THE STATS MEAN?

CATCHES
This is the number of times the keeper has dealt with an attack – usually a cross – by catching the ball.

PENALTIES FACED/SAVED
This is the number of times a goalie has faced a penalty (excludes shoot-outs) and how successful he has been at saving it.

CLEAN SHEETS
Any occasion on which the goalie has not let in a goal for the full duration of the game counts as a clean sheet.

PUNCHES
This is a measure of how often the keeper has dealt with a dangerous ball (usually a cross) by punching it clear.

GOALS CONCEDED
This is the number of goals the keeper has conceded in their career in top-division football.

SAVES
This shows how many times the goalkeeper has stopped a shot or header that was on target.

Did you know?

Goalkeepers can, in theory, score goals with their hands. If they throw a ball downfield and it goes directly into the opposition net, the goal will count but, of course, the ball would have to travel 90+ metres, which is unlikely.

NATIONALITY
Brazil

CURRENT CLUB
Liverpool

ALISSON

The Brazilian has proved to be a top keeper at Liverpool. Alisson is a superb shot-stopper and great at dealing with crosses. Incredibly quick off his line to foil any threat, he can turn defence into attack by finding team-mates with long or short passes.

DATE OF BIRTH	02/10/1992
POSITION	GOALKEEPER
HEIGHT	1.93 M
PRO DEBUT	2013
PREFERRED FOOT	RIGHT

- GOALS CONCEDED: 357
- APPEARANCES: 386
- PENALTIES SAVED: 5
- SAVES: 1,024
- CLEAN SHEETS: 163
- PENALTIES FACED: 29
- CATCHES: 66
- PUNCHES: 175

MAJOR CLUB HONOURS
- Premier League: 2020, 2025
- UEFA Champions League: 2019, runner-up 2022
- FIFA Club World Cup: 2019
- FA Cup: 2022

INTERNATIONAL HONOURS
- Copa América: 2019, runner-up 2021

ACTIVITY AREAS

THIBAUT COURTOIS

Thibaut Courtois uses his height to dominate his penalty area, catching crosses and punching well. An agile shot-stopper, he can get down low to make saves, communicates well with his defence, is excellent coming off his line and passes well.

NATIONALITY
Belgium

CURRENT CLUB
Real Madrid

DATE OF BIRTH	11/05/1992
POSITION	GOALKEEPER
HEIGHT	1.99 M
PRO DEBUT	2009
PREFERRED FOOT	LEFT

- GOALS CONCEDED: 502
- APPEARANCES: 542
- PENALTIES SAVED: 9
- CLEAN SHEETS: 225
- SAVES: 1,391
- PENALTIES FACED: 51
- CATCHES: 131
- PUNCHES: 157

MAJOR CLUB HONOURS
⚽ La Liga: 2014 (At. Mad.), 2020, 2022, runner-up 2023, 2024 ⚽ Prem. League: 2015, 2017 (all Chelsea) ⚽ UEFA Champ. League: 2022, 2024 ⚽ UEFA Europa League: 2012 (At. Mad.) ⚽ FIFA Club World Cup: 2018 ⚽ UEFA Super Cup: 2012 (At. Mad.) 2022 ⚽ Copa del Rey: 2013 (At Mad), 2023

INTERNATIONAL HONOURS
⚽ FIFA World Cup: third place 2018

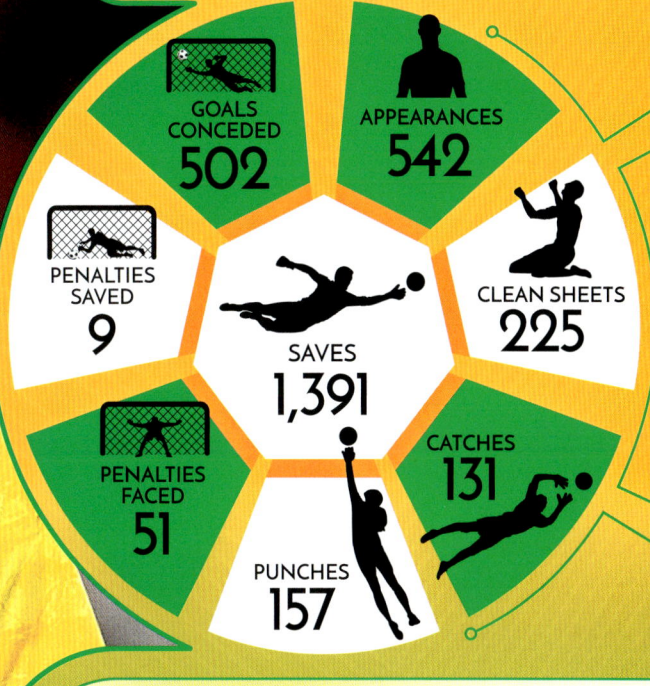

ACTIVITY AREAS

99

NATIONALITY
Italy

CURRENT CLUB
Paris Saint-Germain

GIANLUIGI DONNARUMMA

The Italian is an amazing talent who became a first-team regular at the age of 16. Ten years later, he remains one of the world's best. Mentally strong, Donnarumma dominates his penalty area; he is brave at the feet of forwards, strong in the air and an excellent shot-stopper.

DATE OF BIRTH	25/02/1999
POSITION	GOALKEEPER
HEIGHT	1.96 M
PRO DEBUT	2015
PREFERRED FOOT	RIGHT

- GOALS CONCEDED: 395
- APPEARANCES: 375
- CLEAN SHEETS: 117
- CATCHES: 55
- PUNCHES: 172
- PENALTIES FACED: 50
- PENALTIES SAVED: 11
- SAVES: 1,085

MAJOR CLUB HONOURS
⚽ Ligue 1: 2022, 2023, 2024, 2025 ⚽ UEFA Champions League: 2025 ⚽ FIFA World Club Cup: runner-up 2025 ⚽ Coupe de France: 2024 ⚽ Supercoppa Italiana: 2016 (AC Milan)

INTERNATIONAL HONOURS
⚽ UEFA European Championship: 2020 (2021)
⚽ UEFA Nations League: third place 2021, third place 2023

ACTIVITY AREAS

EDERSON

Owing to his range of passing and great ball skills, Ederson is often considered a playmaker goalkeeper and counted as one of the best in the English Premier League. He is a fine shot-stopper with a reputation for being a great penalty-kick saver, too.

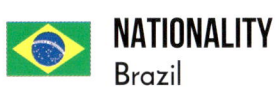

NATIONALITY
Brazil

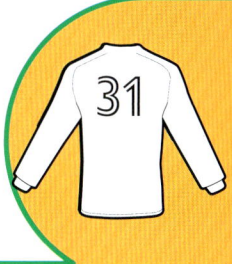

CURRENT CLUB
Manchester City

31

DATE OF BIRTH	17/08/1993
POSITION	GOALKEEPER
HEIGHT	1.88 M
PRO DEBUT	2011
PREFERRED FOOT	LEFT

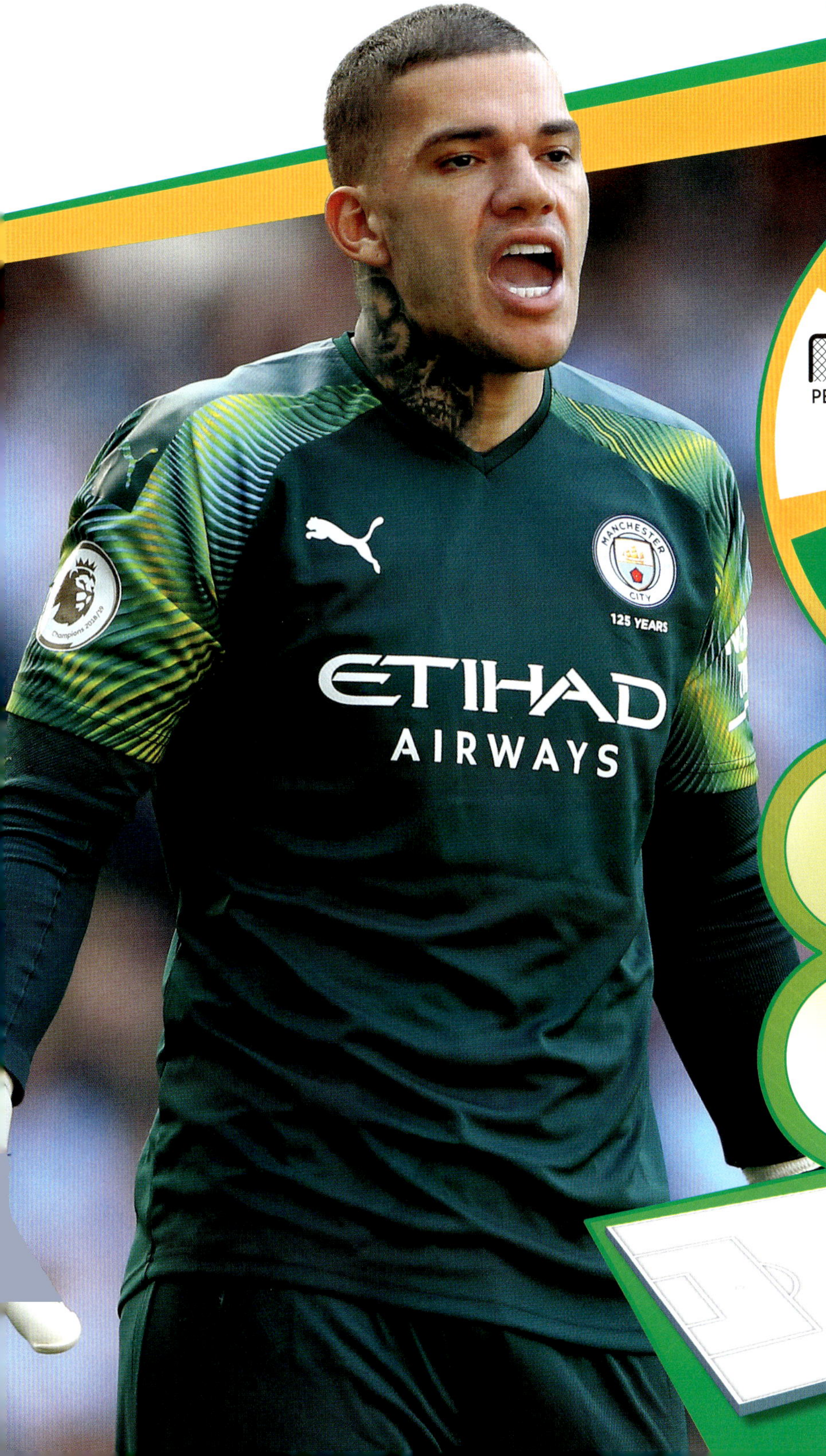
125 YEARS
ETIHAD
AIRWAYS

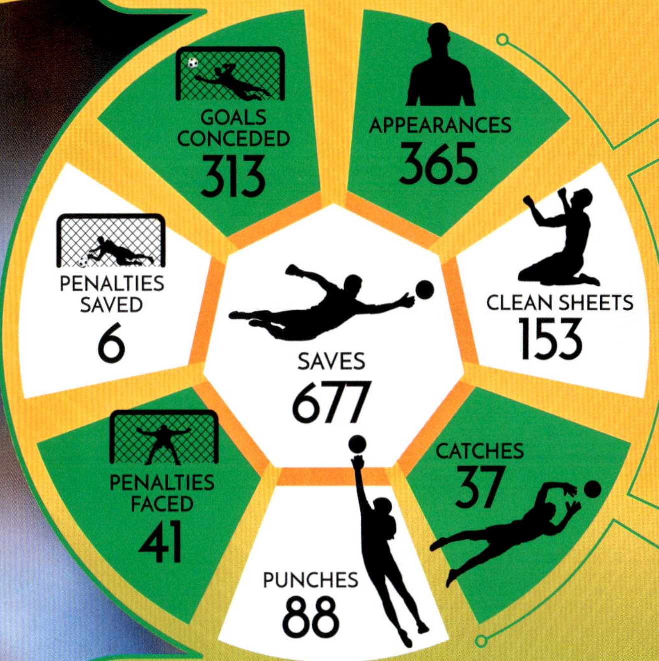
GOALS CONCEDED
313
APPEARANCES
365
PENALTIES SAVED
6
SAVES
677
CLEAN SHEETS
153
PENALTIES FACED
41
PUNCHES
88
CATCHES
37

MAJOR CLUB HONOURS

- Premier League: 2018, 2019, 2021, 2022, 2023, 2024
- UEFA Champions League: runner-up 2021, 2023
- FA Cup: 2019, 2023, runner-up 2024, runner-up 2025
- FIFA Club World Cup: 2023

INTERNATIONAL HONOURS

- Copa América: 2019, runner-up 2021

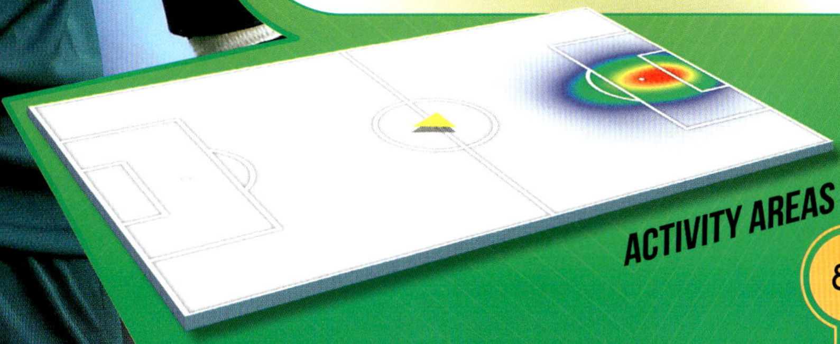

ACTIVITY AREAS

PÉTER GULÁCSI

NATIONALITY Hungary
CURRENT CLUB RB Leipzig

Péter Gulácsi is dedicated to preparing for every football situation he faces. He studies approaching forwards to get an instinct for where they are going to shoot, gets into the right position and then makes difficult saves look very easy.

DATE OF BIRTH	06/05/1990
POSITION	GOALKEEPER
HEIGHT	1.91 M
PRO DEBUT	2008
PREFERRED FOOT	RIGHT

- GOALS CONCEDED: 384
- APPEARANCES: 316
- PENALTIES SAVED: 4
- CLEAN SHEETS: 97
- SAVES: 794
- CATCHES: 59
- PENALTIES FACED: 39
- PUNCHES: 91

MAJOR CLUB HONOURS
- Austrian Bundesliga: 2014, 2015 (Red Bull Salzburg)
- Austrian Cup: 2014, 2015 (Red Bull Salzburg)
- DFB-Pokal: runner-up 2019, runner-up 2021*, 2022, 2023

INTERNATIONAL HONOURS
- FIFA U-20 World Cup: third place 2009

ACTIVITY AREAS

LUKAS HRADECKY

Like many goalkeepers, it wasn't until his thirties that Lukas Hradecky reached his peak. He is an excellent shot-stopper with plenty of confidence, decisive when dealing with crosses, and brilliant at organising his penalty area and communicating with defenders.

NATIONALITY
Finland

CURRENT CLUB
Bayer Leverkusen

DATE OF BIRTH	24/11/1989
POSITION	GOALKEEPER
HEIGHT	1.92 M
PRO DEBUT	2008
PREFERRED FOOT	RIGHT

- GOALS CONCEDED: 466
- APPEARANCES: 369
- PENALTIES SAVED: 6
- CLEAN SHEETS: 103
- SAVES: 1,032
- PENALTIES FACED: 42
- CATCHES: 95
- PUNCHES: 127

MAJOR CLUB HONOURS
- Bundesliga: 2024
- DFB Pokal: 2018 (Eintracht Frankfurt), 2024
- UEFA Europa League: runner-up 2024

INTERNATIONAL HONOURS
- Baltic Cup: Runner-up 2012

ACTIVITY AREAS

16

NATIONALITY	France
CURRENT CLUB	AC Milan

MIKE MAIGNAN

Mike Maignan is a super shot-stopper, especially when dealing with close-range efforts, which allow him to show off his reflexes. He is also a great communicator, shows strong leadership skills and is excellent with his distribution.

DATE OF BIRTH	03/07/1995
POSITION	GOALKEEPER
HEIGHT	1.91 M
PRO DEBUT	2012
PREFERRED FOOT	RIGHT

- GOALS CONCEDED: 330
- APPEARANCES: 315
- PENALTIES SAVED: 12
- CLEAN SHEETS: 110
- SAVES: 831
- CATCHES: 40
- PENALTIES FACED: 50
- PUNCHES: 86

MAJOR CLUB HONOURS
- Serie A: 2022
- Ligue 1: 2021 (Lille)

INTERNATIONAL HONOURS
- UEFA Nations League 2021: third place 2025

ACTIVITY AREAS

EMILIANO MARTÍNEZ

An immensely athletic goalkeeper, Emiliano Martínez is capable of reaching shots going into the top corner with either hand. His quick feet mean he gets into good positions not only to make saves but also reduce the angle for shots.

NATIONALITY
Argentina

CURRENT CLUB
TBC

DATE OF BIRTH	02/09/1992
POSITION	GOALKEEPER
HEIGHT	1.95 M
PRO DEBUT	2012
PREFERRED FOOT	RIGHT

- GOALS CONCEDED: 278
- APPEARANCES: 231
- PENALTIES SAVED: 4
- CLEAN SHEETS: 73
- SAVES: 679
- PENALTIES FACED: 24
- CATCHES: 48
- PUNCHES: 30

MAJOR CLUB HONOURS
- FA Cup: 2020 (Arsenal)

INTERNATIONAL HONOURS
- Copa América: 2021, 2024
- FIFA World Cup: 2022
- CONMEBOL-UEFA Cup of Champions: 2022

ACTIVITY AREAS

KEYLOR NAVAS

NATIONALITY Costa Rica

CURRENT CLUB Newell's Old Boys (Argentina)

Keylor Navas is strong, athletic and a fine organiser and shot stopper. Part of the new breed of hyper-aggressive keepers, he has the confidence to play off his lines, even in situations that might call for more restrained positioning. Navas left French club PSG in 2024 after five years.

DATE OF BIRTH	15/12/1986
POSITION	GOALKEEPER
HEIGHT	1.85 M
PRO DEBUT	2005
PREFERRED FOOT	RIGHT

- GOALS CONCEDED: 315
- APPEARANCES: 318
- PENALTIES SAVED: 10
- CLEAN SHEETS: 113
- SAVES: 960
- CATCHES: 62
- PENALTIES FACED: 43
- PUNCHES: 135

MAJOR CLUB HONOURS
- Ligue 1: 2020, '22, '24 (all PSG)
- La Liga: 2017 (R. Madrid)
- UEFA Champions League: 2016, '17, '18 (all R. Mad.) runner-up 2020 (PSG)
- FIFA World Club Cup: 2014, '16, '17, '18 (all R. Mad.)
- UEFA Super Cup: 2017 (R. Mad.)
- Coupe de France: 2020, '21, '24 (all PSG)

INTERNATIONAL HONOURS
- UNCAF Nations Cup: runner-up 2009, runner-up 2011

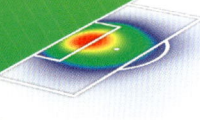
ACTIVITY AREAS

MANUEL NEUER

A top-level keeper for more than 20 years, Manuel Neuer redefined the way goalkeepers play the position, being the original 'sweeper-keeper'. A great distributor, he commands his penalty area and excels as a shot-stopper and organiser.

NATIONALITY Germany

CURRENT CLUB Bayern Munich

DATE OF BIRTH	27/03/1986
POSITION	GOALKEEPER
HEIGHT	1.93 M
PRO DEBUT	2004
PREFERRED FOOT	RIGHT

- GOALS CONCEDED: 583
- APPEARANCES: 675
- PENALTIES SAVED: 12
- CLEAN SHEETS: 295
- SAVES: 1,641
- PENALTIES FACED: 52
- CATCHES: 341
- PUNCHES: 281

MAJOR CLUB HONOURS

⚽ Bundesliga: 2013, 2014, 2015, 2016, 2017, 2018, 2019, 2020, 2021, 2022, 2023, 2025 ⚽ UEFA Champions League: 2013, 2020 ⚽ UEFA Super Cup: 2013, 2020 ⚽ FIFA Club World Cup: 2013, 2020 ⚽ DFB-Pokal 2011 (Schalke 04), 2013, 2014, 2016 2019, 2020

INTERNATIONAL HONOURS

⚽ FIFA World Cup: 2014, third place 2010

ACTIVITY AREAS

JAN OBLAK

NATIONALITY Slovenia
CURRENT CLUB Atlético Madrid

13

One of the world's most agile and accomplished keepers, Jan Oblak is blessed with the quick reflexes to be able to come off his line to snuff out any signs of danger. His communication skills make him adept at organising his defence and taking on the role of team vice-captain.

DATE OF BIRTH	07/01/1993
POSITION	GOALKEEPER
HEIGHT	1.88 M
PRO DEBUT	2009
PREFERRED FOOT	RIGHT

- GOALS CONCEDED: 385
- APPEARANCES: 474
- PENALTIES SAVED: 9
- CLEAN SHEETS: 216
- SAVES: 1,200
- CATCHES: 95
- PENALTIES FACED: 54
- PUNCHES: 131

MAJOR CLUB HONOURS
- La Liga: 2021
- UEFA Champions League: runner-up 2016
- UEFA Europa League: 2018
- UEFA Super Cup: 2018

INTERNATIONAL HONOURS
- None to date

ACTIVITY AREAS

96

RUI PATRÍCIO

Rui Patrício is an old-fashioned continental goalkeeper, primarily a shot-stopper who allows his defenders to deal with crosses into the danger area. He is an expert at coming off his line to narrow angles. Coming to the end of his career, in late May 2025, Patrício signed a short-term deal with UAE Pro League side Al Ain.

NATIONALITY Portugal

CURRENT CLUB Al Ain (UAE)

DATE OF BIRTH	15/02/1988
POSITION	GOALKEEPER
HEIGHT	1.90 M
PRO DEBUT	2006
PREFERRED FOOT	LEFT

- GOALS CONCEDED: 379
- APPEARANCES: 319
- PENALTIES SAVED: 6
- CLEAN SHEETS: 99
- SAVES: 816
- PENALTIES FACED: 37
- CATCHES: 79
- PUNCHES: 61

MAJOR CLUB HONOURS
⚽ Europa Conference League: 2022 (Roma) ⚽ UEFA Europa League: runner-up 2023 ⚽ Taça de Portugal: 2007, 2008, 2015 (Sporting Clube)

INTERNATIONAL HONOURS
⚽ UEFA European Championship: 2016
⚽ UEFA Nations League: 2019

ACTIVITY AREAS

JORDAN PICKFORD

NATIONALITY England
CURRENT CLUB Everton

Playing for one of the lesser teams in the English Premier League, Jordan Pickford is kept busy and is an excellent shot-stopper. Not the tallest of goalkeepers, he prefers to punch rather than catch the ball and is also very good at distributing to team-mates to initiate attacks.

DATE OF BIRTH	07/03/1994
POSITION	GOALKEEPER
HEIGHT	1.85 M
PRO DEBUT	2011
PREFERRED FOOT	LEFT

- GOALS CONCEDED: 472
- APPEARANCES: 327
- PENALTIES SAVED: 7
- CLEAN SHEETS: 87
- SAVES: 1,040
- PENALTIES FACED: 39
- CATCHES: 50
- PUNCHES: 170

MAJOR CLUB HONOURS
- None to date

INTERNATIONAL HONOURS
- UEFA European Championship: runner-up 2020, runner-up 2024
- UEFA Natiom League: third place 2019

ACTIVITY AREAS

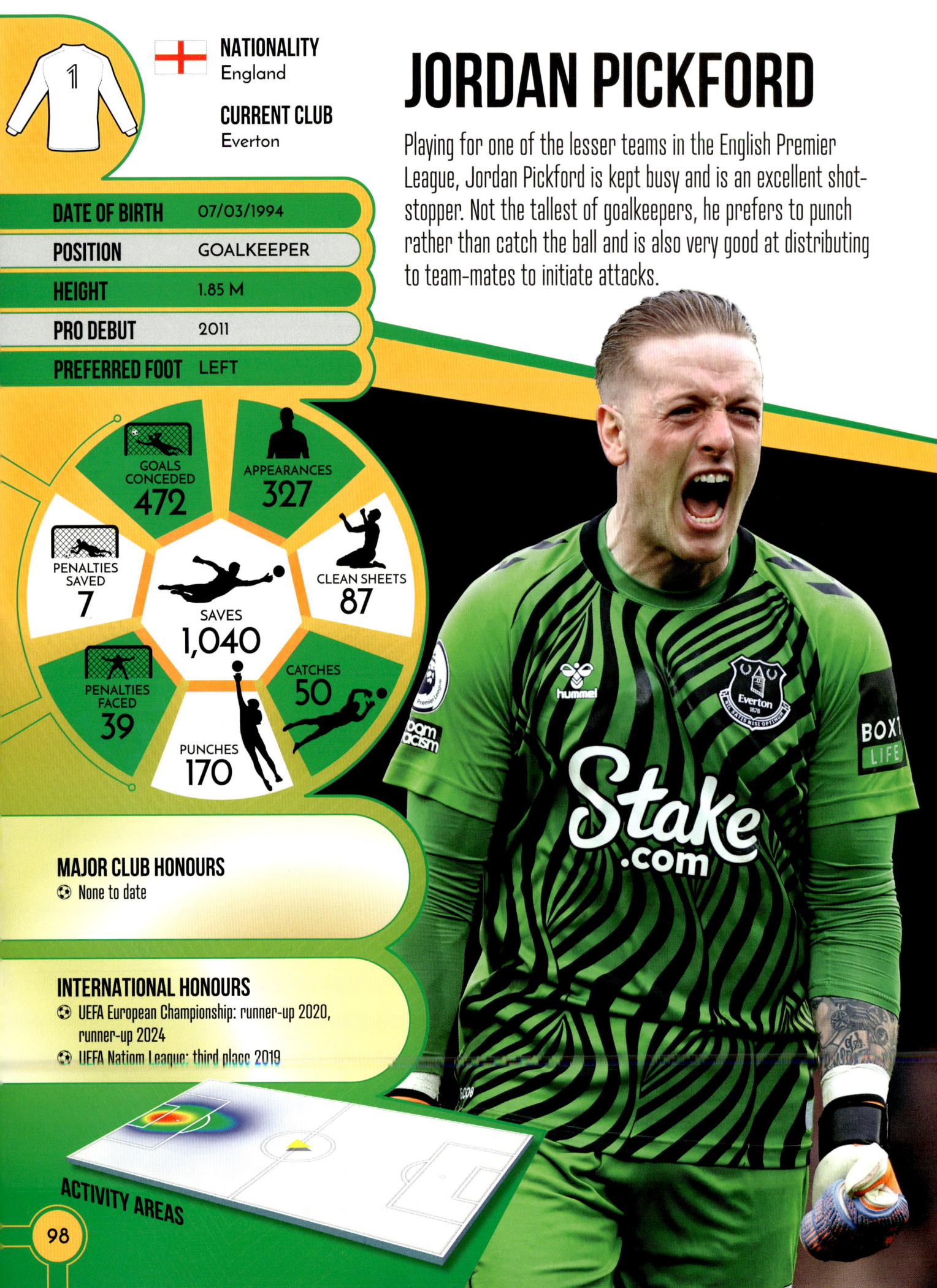

DAVID RAYA

David Raya dominates his penalty area, not only in dealing with crosses, but also his improved technique on the ball allows his defenders to play higher up the pitch. He has fine anticipation and is a top shot-stopper, too.

NATIONALITY
Spain

CURRENT CLUB
Arsenal

DATE OF BIRTH	15/09/1995
POSITION	GOALKEEPER
HEIGHT	1.83 M
PRO DEBUT	2014
PREFERRED FOOT	RIGHT

- GOALS CONCEDED: 147
- APPEARANCES: 154
- PENALTIES SAVED: 3
- CLEAN SHEETS: 59
- SAVES: 413
- PENALTIES FACED: 17
- CATCHES: 30
- PUNCHES: 36

MAJOR CLUB HONOURS
- Premier League: runner-up 2024, runner-up 2025

INTERNATIONAL HONOURS
- UEFA European Championship: 2024
- UEFA Nations League: 2023 runner-up 2025

ACTIVITY AREAS

BRICE SAMBA

NATIONALITY France
CURRENT CLUB Rennes

Brice Samba has the personality and physique to dominate his penalty area. His attributes include stopping shots from both long- and close-range, dealing with crosses and starting attacks with kicks downfield. He is not afraid to make unorthodox saves either.

DATE OF BIRTH	25/04/1994
POSITION	GOALKEEPER
HEIGHT	1.87 M
PRO DEBUT	2011
PREFERRED FOOT	LEFT

- GOALS CONCEDED: 176
- APPEARANCES: 153
- PENALTIES SAVED: 5
- CLEAN SHEETS: 53
- SAVES: 493
- PENALTIES FACED: 29
- CATCHES: 28
- PUNCHES: 24

MAJOR CLUB HONOURS
- None to date

INTERNATIONAL HONOURS
- UEFA Nations League: third place 2025

ACTIVITY AREAS

ROBERT SÁNCHEZ

Robert Sánchez is an agile shot-stopper who also is excellent at communicating with his back four to help play the ball out of defence. He has the unique ability to leave it until the last moment to come off his line, making it more difficult for opponents to get the shot past him.

NATIONALITY
Spain

CURRENT CLUB
Chelsea

DATE OF BIRTH	18/11/1997
POSITION	GOALKEEPER
HEIGHT	1.97 M
PRO DEBUT	2018
PREFERRED FOOT	RIGHT

- GOALS CONCEDED: 159
- APPEARANCES: 136
- PENALTIES SAVED: 3
- CLEAN SHEETS: 40
- SAVES: 364
- PENALTIES FACED: 21
- CATCHES: 16
- PUNCHES: 33

MAJOR CLUB HONOURS
- FIFA World Club Cup: 2025
- UEFA Conference League: 2025
- EFL Cup: runner-up: 2024

INTERNATIONAL HONOURS
- UEFA Nations League: runner-up 2021

ACTIVITY AREAS

YANN SOMMER

NATIONALITY Switzerland
CURRENT CLUB Inter Milan

Yann Sommer is not tall for a goalkeeper but he has great anticipation, reflexes and footwork which more than make up for his lack of height. A good shot-stopper, he is very comfortable playing as a sweeper-keeper, too.

DATE OF BIRTH	17/12/1988
POSITION	GOALKEEPER
HEIGHT	1.83 M
PRO DEBUT	2005
PREFERRED FOOT	LEFT

- GOALS CONCEDED: 577
- APPEARANCES: 455
- PENALTIES SAVED: 7
- CLEAN SHEETS: 140
- SAVES: 1,466
- PENALTIES FACED: 66
- CATCHES: 170
- PUNCHES: 152

MAJOR CLUB HONOURS
- Serie A: 2024
- UEFA Champions League: runner-up 2025
- Bundesliga: 2023 (Bayern Munich)

INTERNATIONAL HONOURS
- None to date

ACTIVITY AREAS

WOJCIECH SZCZĘSNY

Wojciech Szczęsny has grown into one of Europe's most consistent keepers. A natural shot-stopper with lightning reflexes, he is also great at controlling his penalty area, dealing with crosses and setting up counter-attacks with quick clearances.

NATIONALITY
Poland

CURRENT CLUB
Barcelona

DATE OF BIRTH	18/04/1990
POSITION	GOALKEEPER
HEIGHT	1.95 M
PRO DEBUT	2009
PREFERRED FOOT	RIGHT

- GOALS CONCEDED 526
- APPEARANCES 503
- PENALTIES SAVED 16
- CLEAN SHEETS 183
- SAVES 1,307
- PENALTIES FACED 81
- CATCHES 208
- PUNCHES 197

MAJOR CLUB HONOURS
⚽ La Liga: 2025 ⚽ Serie A: 2018, 2019, 2020 (all Juventus) ⚽ Copa del Rey: 2025 ⚽ FA Cup: 2014, 2015 (all Arsenal) ⚽ Coppa Italia: 2018, 2021, 2024 (all Juventus) ⚽

INTERNATIONAL HONOURS
⚽ None to date

ACTIVITY AREAS

MANAGERS

Head coaches are as different from each other as players who play in different positions. But the majority of the 12 featured in this section have one thing in common: they are all winners, either in their domestic leagues or in continental competitions. Some, such as Mikel Arteta, were successful players themselves and trophy winners well before they entered management, while others, such as Claudio Ranieri, had less fruitful playing careers but have had great success as the brains behind a top side.

WHAT DO THE STATS MEAN?

GAMES MANAGED
This is the number of matches the coach has been in charge of across their entire career in football management.

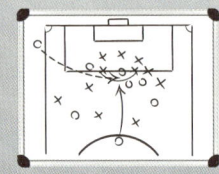
TEAMS MANAGED
The number of clubs (first teams only) that the coach has managed during their career to date.

WINS
This is the number of games the coach has won, including one leg of a cup-tie, even if the tie was lost on aggregate or penalties.

TROPHIES
The trophy list features the head coach's success in domestic top divisions, national and league cups and international club competitions, except any super cups.

Did you know?

Eddie Howe coached Premier League team Newcastle United to their first domestic cup win for 70 years and first of any type for 56 years. He was also the first English manager in 17 years to win a domestic trophy.

XABI ALONSO

Xabi Alonso is Europe's most in-demand coach after winning the Bundesliga title in his first full season. His teams play 3–4–2–1 formation, inviting pressure, then counter-attacking and taking advantage of holes in the opposition's defences.

NATIONALITY
Spain

CURRENT CLUB
Real Madrid

YEARS AS HEAD COACH: 6

FIRST CLUB: REAL SOCIEDAD B

CLUBS MANAGED	GAMES	LEAGUE TITLES
2	237	1

WINS	DRAW	LOSSES
127	56	54

CHAMPIONS LEAGUE TROPHIES	EUROPA LEAGUE TROPHIES	OTHER TROPHIES*
0	0	2

*Excludes Super Cups

MAJOR CLUB HONOURS
- Bundesliga: 2024 (Bayer Leverkusen)
- DFB-Pokal: 2024 (Bayer Leverkusen)
- UEFA Europa League: runner-up 2024 (Bayer Leverkusen)

CARLO ANCELOTTI

The vastly experienced and accomplished Carlo Ancelotti uses different systems depending on the opposition and players available. His favourite formation is 4–4–2, sometimes in a diamond, other times with four midfielders in a line across the pitch.

NATIONALITY
Italy

CURRENT TEAM
Brazil

YEARS AS HEAD COACH: 30

FIRST CLUB: REGGIANA

CLUBS MANAGED	GAMES	LEAGUE TITLES
10	1,401	6

WINS	DRAW	LOSSES
838	306	257

CHAMPIONS LEAGUE TROPHIES	EUROPA LEAGUE TROPHIES	OTHER TROPHIES*
5	0	19

*Excludes Super Cups

MAJOR CLUB HONOURS
- La Liga: 2022, runner-up 2023, 2024 (all Real Madrid)
- UEFA Champions League: 2003, 2007 (all AC Milan), 2014, 2022, 2024 (all Real Madrid)
- FIFA Club World Cup: 2007 (AC Milan), 2014, 2022 (all Real Madrid)
- Serie A: 2004 (AC Milan)
- Premier League: 2010 (Chelsea)
- Ligue 1: 2013 (Paris St-Germain)
- Copa del Rey: 2014, 2023 (all R. Mad.)
- Coppa Italia: 2003 (AC Milan)
- Bundesliga: 2017 (Bayern Munich)

MIKEL ARTETA

Mikel Arteta gambled on taking a high-profile club as his first job in management. He changed his style from a defensively strong 5—4—1 to a more aggressive attacking 4—2—3—1, with players causing danger from anywhere on the pitch.

NATIONALITY
Spain

CURRENT CLUB
Arsenal

YEARS AS HEAD COACH: 6

FIRST CLUB: ARSENAL

CLUBS MANAGED	GAMES	LEAGUE TITLES
1	290	0

WINS	DRAW	LOSSES
169	55	66

CHAMPIONS LEAGUE TROPHIES	EUROPA LEAGUE TROPHIES	OTHER TROPHIES*
0	0	3

*Excludes Super Cups

MAJOR CLUB HONOURS
- Premier League: runner-up 2023, runner-up 2024, runner-up 2025
- FA Cup: 2020
- FA Community Shield: 2020, 2023

UNAI EMERY

Unai Emery has enjoyed great success managing clubs that have a modest budget. His preference is either a 4—2—3—1 formation or 4—4—2, the choice dependent on the attacking skills of the two central midfielders and their ability to retain possession.

NATIONALITY
Spain

CURRENT CLUB
Aston Villa

YEARS AS HEAD COACH: 21

FIRST CLUB: LORCA DEPORTIVA

CLUBS MANAGED	GAMES	LEAGUE TITLES
9	1,066	1

WINS	DRAW	LOSSES
569	231	266

CHAMPIONS LEAGUE TROPHIES	EUROPA LEAGUE TROPHIES	OTHER TROPHIES*
0	4	6

*Excludes Super Cups

MAJOR CLUB HONOURS
- UEFA Europa League: 2014, 2015, 2016 (all Sevilla), 2021 (Villareal), runner-up 2019 (Arsenal)
- Ligue 1: 2018 (Paris Saint-Germain)
- Coupe de France: 2017, 2018 (all Paris Saint-Germain)

LUIS ENRIQUE

Luis Enrique will not compromise his football beliefs, and he will play in the formation that suits his available players, normally 4–3–3 or 3–4–3. He wants his players to express themselves on the ball whenever possible.

NATIONALITY Spain

CURRENT CLUB Paris Saint-Germain

YEARS AS HEAD COACH: 14

FIRST CLUB: BARCELONA B

CLUBS MANAGED	GAMES	LEAGUE TITLES
5	498	4

WINS	DRAW	LOSSES
306	98	94

CHAMPIONS LEAGUE TROPHIES	EUROPA LEAGUE TROPHIES	OTHER TROPHIES*
2	0	9

*Excludes Super Cups

MAJOR CLUB HONOURS
- UEFA Champions League: 2015 (Barcelona), 2025
- Ligue 1: 2024, 2025
- La Liga: 2015, 2016 (all Barcelona)
- FIFA World Club Cup: 2015 (Barcelona), runner-up 2025
- Coupe de France: 2024, 2025
- Copa del Rey: 2015, 2016, 2017 (all Barcelona)

HANSI FLICK

Hansi Flick won many medals and trophies as a player, then as assistant coach and head coach at Bayern Munich. He's also managed the German national team. His teams focus on playing high-pressing, attacking football.

NATIONALITY Germany

CURRENT CLUB Barcelona

YEARS AS HEAD COACH: 29

FIRST CLUB: VICTORIA BAMMENTAL

CLUBS MANAGED	GAMES	LEAGUE TITLES
4	146	3

WINS	DRAW	LOSSES
114	16	16

CHAMPIONS LEAGUE TROPHIES	EUROPA LEAGUE TROPHIES	OTHER TROPHIES*
1	0	6

*Excludes Super Cups

MAJOR CLUB HONOURS
- La Liga: 2025
- Bundesliga: 2020, 2021 all (Bayern Munich)
- UEFA Champions League: 2020 (Bayern Munich)
- Copa del Rey: 2025
- DFB-Pokal: 2020 (Bayern Munich)
- FIFA Club World Cup: 2020 (Bayern Munich)
- UEFA Super Cup: 2020 (Bayern Munich)

GIAN PIERO GASPERINI

Gian Piero Gasperini wants his teams to be attacking, but to defend man-for-man when not in possession. His 3—4—3 formation is fluid; when his teams attack, the wing-backs play as wide midfielders and try to outnumber opposing defenders.

NATIONALITY
Italy

CURRENT CLUB
Roma

YEARS AS HEAD COACH: 22

FIRST CLUB: CROTONE

CLUBS MANAGED	GAMES	LEAGUE TITLES
5	874	0

WINS	DRAW	LOSSES
402	209	263

CHAMPIONS LEAGUE TROPHIES	EUROPA LEAGUE TROPHIES	OTHER TROPHIES*
0	1	0

*Excludes Super Cups

MAJOR CLUB HONOURS
- UEFA Europa League: 2024

PEP GUARDIOLA

Once a great midfielder himself, Pep Guardiola devised the *tika-taka* passing system at Barcelona (from 2008 to '12). Disciplined in possession, without the ball his teams press the opposition into making mistakes and then launch rapid counter-attacks.

NATIONALITY
Spain

CURRENT CLUB
Manchester City

YEARS AS HEAD COACH: 17

FIRST CLUB: BARCELONA B

CLUBS MANAGED	GAMES	LEAGUE TITLES
4	979	12

WINS	DRAW	LOSSES
701	154	124

CHAMPIONS LEAGUE TROPHIES	EUROPA LEAGUE TROPHIES	OTHER TROPHIES*
3	0	24

*Excludes Super Cups

MAJOR CLUB HONOURS
- Premier League: 2018, 2019, 2021, 2022, 2023, 2024
- UEFA Champions League: 2009, 2011 Barcelona), runner-up 2021, 2023
- FIFA Club World Cup: 2009, 2011 (Barcelona), 2013 (B. Munich)
- La Liga: 2009, 2010, 2011 (Barcelona)
- Bundesliga: 2014, 2015, 2016 (B. Munich)
- FA Cup: 2019, 2023, Runner-up 2024, runner-up 2025

EDDIE HOWE

Eddie Howe's reputation has improved dramatically, and he is now considered an elite head coach. He prefers a 4–3–3 formation in possession, and 4–5–1 without the ball, stressing pressure on the opposing defenders, to force quick turnovers.

NATIONALITY
England

CURRENT CLUB
Newcastle United

YEARS AS HEAD COACH: 17

FIRST CLUB: AFC BOURNEMOUTH

CLUBS MANAGED	GAMES	LEAGUE TITLES
3	718	0

WINS	DRAW	LOSSES
316	151	251

CHAMPIONS LEAGUE TROPHIES	EUROPA LEAGUE TROPHIES	OTHER TROPHIES*
0	0	1

MAJOR CLUB HONOURS
- EFL Cup: runner-up 2023, 2025

*Excludes Super Cups

SIMONE INZAGHI

Simone Inzaghi's teams almost always play in a 3–5–2 formation. He likes his team to keep possession with short passes, patiently waiting to strike, and encourages his central defenders to draw opponents out of position to join attacks.

NATIONALITY
Italy

CURRENT CLUB
Al Hillal (Saudi Arabia)

YEARS AS HEAD COACH: 10

FIRST CLUB: LAZIO

CLUBS MANAGED	GAMES	LEAGUE TITLES
3	468	1

WINS	DRAW	LOSSES
275	86	107

CHAMPIONS LEAGUE TROPHIES	EUROPA LEAGUE TROPHIES	OTHER TROPHIES*
0	0	8

MAJOR CLUB HONOURS
- Serie A: 2024
- UEFA Champions League: runner-up 2023, runner-up 2025
- Coppa Italia: 2019 (Lazio), 2022, 2023

*Excludes Super Cups

DIEGO SIMEONE

Diego Simeone likes to use a formation which is almost a 4–2–2–2 unit, with wide midfielders playing between the two central ones and the strikers. Strong defensively, his teams are great at defending set pieces and dangerous in attack.

NATIONALITY
Argentina

CURRENT CLUB
Atlético Madrid

YEARS AS HEAD COACH: 18

FIRST CLUB: RACING CLUB

CLUBS MANAGED	GAMES	LEAGUE TITLES
7	941	4

WINS	DRAW	LOSSES
531	215	195

CHAMPIONS LEAGUE TROPHIES	EUROPA LEAGUE TROPHIES	OTHER TROPHIES*
0	2	4

*Excludes Super Cups

MAJOR CLUB HONOURS
- UEFA Champions League: runner-up 2014, 2016
- UEFA Europa League: 2012, 2018
- UEFA Super Cup: 2012, 2018
- La Liga: 2014, 2021
- Copa del Rey: 2013
- Primera División Apertura 2006 (Estudiantes)
- Primera División Clausura 2008 (Racing Club)

ARNE SLOT

Arne Slot is an astute and innovative coach. He has a reputation for developing young players and playing attractive, attacking football in a 4–3–3 formation. He sometimes operates a 4–2–3–1 lineup, with two midfielders in front of the back four.

NATIONALITY
Netherlands

CURRENT CLUB
Liverpool

YEARS AS HEAD COACH: 9

FIRST CLUB: SC CAMBUUR

CLUBS MANAGED	GAMES	LEAGUE TITLES
4	298	2

WINS	DRAW	LOSSES
189	60	49

CHAMPIONS LEAGUE TROPHIES	EUROPA LEAGUE TROPHIES	OTHER TROPHIES*
0	0	1

*Excludes Super Cups

MAJOR CLUB HONOURS
- Premier League: 2025
- Eredivisie: 2023 (Feyenoord)
- KNVB Cup: 2024 (Feyenoord)
- UEFA Europa Conference: 2022 (Feyenoord)

NOTES